Suffering – Conversations Old & New

"In this clear, courageous, and deeply human book, Jon Herrin, in his wisdom and deep compassion, invites us into an honest and grace-filled conversation that reframes the question of suffering with honesty and hope. Through Job's story and his friend's lived experience, this gifted author reveals a God who is present, compassionate, and never the source of our pain."
—Bishop Cynthia Fierro Harvey, Rio Texas and Texas Annual Conferences of the United Methodist Church

"Herrin provides for us a positive and accessible deep dive into Job that helps us respond to those who suffer and grieve with deeper understanding and tenderness."
—Robert Schnase, retired United Methodist Bishop, author of *Five Practices of Fruitful Living* and *Practicing Extravagant Generosity*

"I have long been struck by Job's devastating suffering, the role of his 'friends,' and the power of his encounter with the living God. In the midst of a real-life world that cries out in pain, Jon Herrin's book guides us to wisdom and hope."
—Bishop Laura Merrill, Arkansas, Oklahoma, Oklahoma Indian Missionary Conferences of the United Methodist Church

"Pastoral care teaches us that the more we talk about suffering, the more we process in healthy ways, the more we can see God walking along side. I am grateful for Jon and his healthy approach of acknowledging suffering and giving people space to process their journey."
—Rev. Dr. Robert Lopez, Vice President Pastoral Care, Methodist Healthcare

"I needed this book the night I stood in the ER beside parents whose toddler had drowned. They needed it in the following months of "Why?" Academically solid, Herrin writes pastorally and accessibly for all who seek to understand where God is in human suffering."
 —Rev. Pamela Dykehouse, South District Superintendent, Rio Texas Conference of the UMC.

"Herrin writes with the depth and wisdom of a teacher and the sensitive heart of a pastor. His work navigates the biblical spirituality of human suffering, giving life to an honest and practical text, indispensable for the challenges facing Wesleyan pastoral ministry in the 21st century."
 —Rev. Jaser Dávila, Judah District Superintendent, Methodist Church of Mexico

"In this book, Herrin aims to help us understand 'why suffering exists and how to live with it in our lives.' Read it, and in the end, you will receive a balm that will give meaning to your own pain and that of those around you!"
 —Rev. Raúl García de Ochoa, former bishop of the Eastern Annual Conference of the Methodist Church of Mexico.

SUFFERING

CONVERSATIONS OLD & NEW

Reading Job in the 21ˢᵗ Century

Jon A. Herrin

Border Life Press
Mission, Texas

Copyright© 2025 by Jon A. Herrin
All rights reserved

Published by **Border Life Press**
Mission, Texas United States of America
borderlifepress@gmail.com

Paperback and eBook produced through Kindle Direct Publishing.

All rights reserved. Except for brief quotations (less than 100 words), no part of this work may be reproduced, copied, or used in any way without the written permission of the author.

Unless otherwise indicated, all Scripture quotations are taken from the Holy Bible, New International Version®, NIV® Copyright ©1973, 1978, 1984, 2011 by Biblica, Inc.® Used by permission. All rights reserved worldwide.

ISBN: 979-8-9934481-1-4

DEDICATION

For those who have shared my suffering and those who allowed me into their suffering.

And for Vania—who invited me into her suffering, whose conversations pushed me to write this book, who continues to teach me about suffering.

ACKNOWLEDGMENTS

I am grateful to all who have sat and walked, listened and talked with me through my seasons of suffering, and for those who encouraged me to write. Especially—

My wife, Jeanne

Mom & Papa

Tommy Housworth

Teri Bradshaw Hannah

Fr. Gary Young

CONTENTS

Preface i

Outline of Job vii

Chapter 1 – Introducing Job 1

Chapter 2 – Beginning at the End – Job 1:1-22 7

Chapter 3 – "You Give and Take Away" – Job 1:21 21

Chapter 4 – Being a Friend – Job 2:1-13 37

Chapter 5 – Getting it All Out – Job 3:1-26 53

Chapter 6 – "With Friends Like These…" – Job 4-13 69

Chapter 7 – Hope = Life! – Job 14:7-15 81

Chapter 8 – Job Questions Reality – Job 15-31 95

Chapter 9 – Job Begins to Understand – Job 31:35-37 105

Chapter 10 – God Speaks and Job Listens…and Learns –
Job 41:1-11 119

Chapter 11 – Questions Remain – Job 42:7-17 129

Chapter 12 – Closing Thoughts—God with Us 143

Bibliography 151

About the Author 155

PREFACE

Job—the book of the Bible and the person who gives the book its name—has been the subject of books, articles, essays, poems, paintings, drawings, and woodcuts as people have been fascinated by and wrestled with the issues of both suffering and the sovereignty of a good God.

Some of my early childhood memories include the images in children's Bibles and Sunday School materials of Job sitting in a pile of ashes scraping the runny sores of his arms and legs with a shard of broken pottery. I am certain that some of the details of this incident of Job's life were garishly amplified by imaginative teachers and preachers along the way. While that is a rather 'minor' moment in the greater story, that is the image that first comes to my mind when I hear "Job."

Years later, as an adult, as a pastor, I found myself serving a congregation in Rio Grande City, Texas, on the US/Mexico border, and the sermon lectionary[1] I was following at that time called (or allowed) for a summer preaching series on Job. I had never really preached through Job, and I was a bit reluctant to take it on—I had wrestled with my own share of suffering and had all but given up attempting to reconcile the ideas of the 'sovereignty of God' and the goodness of God with the horrors of our world. I had decided,

---

[1] Narrative Lectionary, produced by Luther Seminary, St. Paul, MN. See: http://www.workingpreacher.org/narrative_faqs.aspx

"Well, there are some things we just can't thoroughly understand on this side of eternity ..." (like the Trinity!).

But, after some reflection and following my usual readiness to take on a challenge, I decided to give Job a go, to preach at least a couple of sermons from the first chapters to see what might happen. The gauntlet was thrown down, and the challenge was on! I began to read again—after many years—the words of Job, and I found the text speaking in new and amazing ways, revealing God's will, power, sovereignty, and grace. And, I began to learn more about Job—the book and the person.

At that time in my ministry, I had recently taken up the practice of writing out my sermons in manuscript form. The six-week sermon series that came out of that season has evolved into the substantially expanded work you now hold in hand (or view on your screen.) This work is my own journey of understanding the book of Job in the Old Testament and its message in what I hope may be new and more helpful ways.

More than perhaps ever before, our generation and our time need something to help us understand the world of suffering. In 2020, we encountered COVID-19, the Black Lives Matter movement (that grew out of centuries of suffering), political polarization, and more natural disasters than we in the U.S. had seen in a long time. While there is 'light at the end of the tunnel' with regard to some of these issues, we continue to suffer pain from the pandemic, from racial unrest, political divisions, and increasingly destructive weather patterns as we move through the 2020's (not to mention the "everyday" sorts of suffering that have always afflicted us all: illnesses, broken-hearts, financial pains, and shattered dreams).

This work was further spurred forward because of a serendipitous friendship that began at the end of 2020. As if the issues of suffering mentioned above were not enough, I learned even more when I met a woman named Marjan.[2] Her sister, Malika, had been a professional friend via LinkedIn for several years. Malika and her family had moved from Iran to Canada, and she was anxious to improve her English. As an English teacher, I was interested in both her language-learning adventures and in helping her make sense of North American culture. As a matter of course, we shared stories about our families in our occasional exchanges.

In December of 2020, I heard from Malika—the message was disjointed, desperate. Something had happened. Her sister, Marjan, just 35 years old, had been diagnosed with breast cancer—"invasive ductal carcinoma, poorly differentiated and triple-negative." She was facing months of chemotherapy to be followed by a double mastectomy. Furthermore, I learned that as soon as Marjan's fiancé heard of the diagnosis, he broke off the engagement and left her. She was supposed to begin her final semester of university studies in January. That would not happen now. She would not be able to continue with her job at the bank. Her life—in a 30 minute conversation with her doctor—completely fell apart. I felt as if I were reading the first chapter of Job all over again, only this time the one suffering was not 4000 years and 7000 miles removed. Marjan was close by. She was alone in Los Angeles, California, and the suffering was crushing in on her.

I am a writer and a theologian and an educator, and I am also a minister, a pastor in the Church. My response to Malika's message is just the way I respond to anyone who shares such news with me: Would your sister like to talk to someone? Do you want me to talk to her? Would she be willing to talk with me?

Malika said she would check and get back to me. I went on with my week. On the following Friday, I received the message: "Marjan wants to talk with you."

---

[2] Malika and Marjan are not their real names.

I called Marjan, and our conversation began. She is on a journey through suffering. She is not a person of faith, per se. Her questions are huge, deep, and real. And, our conversations drove me back to the manuscript for this book—a project I had begun two or three years before but had set aside. Marjan became the 'tipping point' for finishing this work. The first iteration came out in 2021 as *A Journey through Suffering: A New Reading of Job in the 21st Century*. This work was well received by hundreds of readers. A number of people asked for a study guide to accompany this "journey through suffering." Since Marjan and I remained in conversation, since others wanted a study guide, and since I continued to contemplate and study the theme of suffering, I determined to release an expanded book on this theme. This is the book you now hold in your hand.

In this new work, I will be sharing parts of our conversations and my reflections of those chats in the chapters of this work. We will see more of Marjan and her suffering. She is living through suffering the likes of which you and I probably have never had to deal with.

But, we have all suffered, we are suffering, and we will suffer. As the author of Ecclesiastes so aptly puts it, "There is nothing new under the sun" (Ecclesiastes 1:9). Suffering seems to be part and parcel of our life on earth. The world suffers. Still, every generation asks the questions: Why? How could this happen under the watch of a loving God? Do we deserve this suffering? Can we avoid suffering? We want answers. While Job the book itself answers some of the questions, I have found that when we read Job in concert with greater message of the Bible, many of the questions are answered.

* * *

In the interest of 'full disclosure,' I am a Christian in the United Methodist tradition, a former international missionary, a former university and seminary professor, and presently a pastor, a husband and father, and a writer. I am all of these things and more than those things in the way we are all more than what we do or have done, more than the 'hats we wear.' All of my life experiences bear on my understanding and presentation of Job in this work—from my birth in the 'deep South,' to growing up as a 'missionary kid' in the Caribbean, to working as an English and theology professor in the US and abroad, to my present work as a pastor, educator, and writer on southern border of the United States.

My wish, my hope, is that the thoughts, narratives, and ideas expressed in these pages will enliven the reader's interest in Job (both the book and person), provide a deeper understanding of God, show clearly where suffering comes from and why we experience it, and encourage all in their determination to make sense of and live through the suffering in our world.

Jon A Herrin
October 2025

AN OUTLINE OF JOB

We provide an outline of Job here for those who are interested in these particularities. This work is not an exhaustive commentary on Job. We will not address or explore every nook and cranny of this book. We are examining selected passages and chapters, summarizing others, and skipping right over some chapters that present nothing 'new' or helpful to our understanding of suffering. (Forcing you to follow through the exegesis of some of those chapters would be suffering in itself!).

I.   Prologue (chs. 1-2)

    A. Meet Job! (ch. 1:1-5)

    B. Satan Challenges God about Job (chs. 1:6 - 2:13)

II.   Dialogues—Disputes: Job, Eliphaz, Bildad, and Zophar (chs. 3-31)

III.   Elihu Joins the Fray (chs. 32-37)

IV.   God and Job (chs. 38:1-42:6)

    A. God speaks (chs. 38:1-40:2)

    B. Job recognizes his place (ch. 40:3-5)

    C. God speaks again (ch. 40:6-41:34)

    D. Job realizes the error of his ways (ch. 42:1-6)

V. Epilogue (ch.42:7-17)

    A. God Corrects Job's "Friends" (ch.42:7-9)

    B. …And Job "lived happily ever after..." (ch. 42:10-17)

Chapter 1
INTRODUCING JOB

I would like to introduce you to Job ... but that is not so easy. The commentary on Job that I have beside me at this moment has a very helpful bibliography page just behind the cover or title page that lets the reader know that the commentary was written by David J.A. Clines, published in 1989 by Zondervan.[1] This page also provides a Library of Congress number and an ISBN (International Standard Book Number). On the back cover of the book, we find out about Clines, the author—his present academic appointment, his academic career, and some selected publications. We can be fairly confident that he is qualified to speak about Job.

The book of Job in our Bibles, just after Ruth and before the Psalms, gives us none of this information. We get the name of the book, the title: Job. And then, the writer—the unnamed, questionably qualified author—dives right into this amazing story or journey: "In the land of Uz there lived a man whose name was Job...."

Job may have been one of the very first books of the Bible to be penned on papyrus or sheep skin. Many scholars today tend to date Job anywhere from around 650 BC back to the 1000's BC—almost

---

[1] David J. A. Clines. *Word Biblical Commentary: Job 1-20*. (Zondervan, 1989).

a thousand years before Christ. Yet, elements of style, content, people groups mentioned, and other internal clues have led still other scholars to suggest that this story actually comes out of the "Patriarchal Period" (the times of Abraham, Isaac, and Jacob)—almost 2000 years before Christ.[2] Either way, this is an old book—one that has obviously stood the test of time.

If we were to know the author by name and address, if we were able to locate this book chronologically in the ancient world, if we were to have the original manuscript complete with ISBN, none of this would change the message of Job. We would still be striving to understand what is going on in this book and how to apply it to our lives and to the world around us.

Each generation tries its hand at making sense of the grand themes of Job: suffering and the sovereignty of God. In seminary, the term used to discuss all of this is "theodicy"—the "defense of God's goodness and omnipotence in view of the existence of evil."[3]

The questions about suffering and divine sovereignty are exactly what led me to accept the challenge of preaching the series of sermons that evolved into this book. I and many others in the congregations I had served and in the classes I had taught had encountered too much suffering. We had lost loved ones to cancer and other illnesses. We had suffered loss of jobs and loss of love. Dreams had been crushed and hopes extinguished.

All of us were in for it as 2020 came along with all of the unexpected happenings of that year: the COVID-19 pandemic; the pulling back of the curtain that had long hidden the systemic racism and the rise of the "Black Lives Matter" movement. We turned the corner in 2021 with hope only to see the political division of our

---

[2] Ibid, lvii.
[3] "Theodicy." *Merriam-Webster.com Dictionary*, Merriam-Webster, https://www.merriam-webster.com/dictionary/theodicy. Accessed 1 May. 2021.

nation come to a head in the storming of the Capitol Building in Washington. Illness, death, loss, racism, storms, wildfires, political unrest, divisions—suffering has revealed itself in living color to all of us in so many ways. We crave answers and hope and direction.

My wife, Jeanne, and I live on the 'southern border' in south Texas—a region that often filled the newscasts in 2020 due to our 'COVID numbers.' In 2019, we were in the news due to the immigration practices of separating parents and children. A few years ago, we held the spotlight due to the massive immigration of young people crossing the border looking for a better life, and that came around yet again in 2021.

This is a region filled with suffering—those seeking to cross the border to escape the horrors of violence and injustice—the suffering—in their own lands, those who have crossed only to be separated from parent or child and locked away until a hearing or something happens, and those who have been here for years but without legal status—their prospects of a "better life" severely limited if not grim overall. And then, Hurricane Hanna blew through in July 2020 and a devastating winter storm hit in February 2021. Why?! Is there no end to the suffering?

Beyond these particular regional issues, the people here in the Rio Grande Valley face exactly the same issues that humans the world over face—lost jobs, unrealized dreams, deaths of loved ones, natural disasters, broken hearts, pains of rejection, injury, disability, loss of wealth. I have faced some of these, and I imagine you have, too.

For all of us, I have longed to find a way to make sense of the pain and suffering of this world. Will Job help us do that? Can we make sense of the suffering?

One of my literary heroes, James Martin, SJ, suggests that trying to make sense of this is impossible. He writes, "The best answer to 'Why do we suffer?' may be 'We don't know.' Anyone who offers you 'the answer' is either a liar or a fool. And has probably never faced real suffering."[4]

When we get to the end of this work, the reader can decide if I am a liar or a fool, and whether or not I know anything about suffering. But more important even than my own experience is what Job can teach us. I am convinced that the book of Job, coupled with the greater story of Scripture, gives us so much that can enable us to understand why suffering exists and how to live through the suffering of our lives.

My friend, Marjan, who knows suffering firsthand, will jump in with us from time to time on this journey. Her questions about her suffering are our questions. Her reactions are the same reactions of so many who suffer. We will learn from Marjan along this journey.

Job helps us know why we suffer, why others suffer, and—perhaps most importantly—what to do with suffering in our lives. Job has much to teach us, and we have much to learn. At the end of each chapter, readers will find a brief section entitled, "On the Journey through Suffering," in which I will summarize our discoveries or insights from the journey. I have also provided "Questions for Reflection" to help the reader think with me through what we find, questions that can be used by individual readers or by small groups who may read this book together. Now, let us see what we can discover and learn as we journey through these the ancient pages of Job in the early 21st Century.

---

[4] James Martin, JS. "Why is There Suffering?" *The Way of Suffering: Readings for an Enlightened Life*. James Leach et al, eds. (Maryknoll, NY: Orbis Books, 2020) 9.

Questions for Reflection—

1. From your own experience and knowledge, why do you think people suffer?

_____

_____

_____

2. Have you known suffering in your own life? What has that looked like?

_____

_____

_____

3. How have you responded to suffering in your life and in the lives of your loved ones?

_____

_____

_____

Chapter 2
BEGINNING AT THE END
JOB 1:1-22

Let us travel back in time in the Old Testament to one of the more often read, best loved, and most perplexing books: Job. Perhaps this journey through Job is a new journey, a new direction for you, moving towards a new destination, a first-time visit to this ancient place; perhaps you are returning yet again to a well visited landmark in your life of faith.

Job the man has himself drawn us in for centuries. We talk about 'the patience of Job,' but do we know where that idea really comes from? And is this truly a story that tells us about Job's patience? We will find out.

Many may know that the book has to do with suffering—something common to us all. This theme of 'suffering' pulls us in—it is a part of the "human condition." We all want to understand suffering, to understand why we have suffering in our lives and learn how to deal with and respond to suffering. And, we want to know how to avoid suffering—if we even can. As humans, we crave explanation—that is what has given birth to every area of study that exists. We want to know 'why?'

Let us begin the journey now into this ancient world to see what this book teaches us about Job, and since we Christians hold that

God inspired the writing of our biblical texts, let us then see what this book teaches us about God ... and about ourselves.

Getting Started...

In order to get the bottom of our questions, we really need to hear again the story of how Job's suffering all began:

> ¹In the land of Uz there lived a man whose name was Job. This man was blameless and upright; he feared God and shunned evil. ²He had seven sons and three daughters, ³and he owned seven thousand sheep, three thousand camels, five hundred yoke of oxen and five hundred donkeys, and had a large number of servants. He was the greatest man among all the people of the East.
> ⁴His sons used to hold feasts in their homes on their birthdays, and they would invite their three sisters to eat and drink with them. ⁵When a period of feasting had run its course, Job would make arrangements for them to be purified. Early in the morning he would sacrifice a burnt offering for each of them, thinking, "Perhaps my children have sinned and cursed God in their hearts." This was Job's regular custom.
> ⁶One day the sons of God came to present themselves before the LORD, and the Adversary—Satan—also came with them. ⁷The LORD said to Satan, "Where have you come from?"
> Satan answered the LORD, "From roaming throughout the earth, going back and forth on it."
> ⁸Then the LORD said to Satan, "Have you considered my servant Job? There is no one on earth like him; he is blameless and upright, a man who fears God and shuns evil."

⁹"Does Job fear God for nothing?" Satan replied.
¹⁰"Have you not put a hedge around him and his household and everything he has? You have blessed the work of his hands, so that his flocks and herds are spread throughout the land. ¹¹But now stretch out your hand and strike everything he has, and he will surely curse you to your face."
¹²The LORD said to Satan, "Very well, then, everything he has is in your power, but on the man himself do not lay a finger."
Then Satan went out from the presence of the LORD.
¹³One day when Job's sons and daughters were feasting and drinking wine at the oldest brother's house, ¹⁴a messenger came to Job and said, "The oxen were plowing and the donkeys were grazing nearby, ¹⁵and the Sabeans attacked and made off with them. They put the servants to the sword, and I am the only one who has escaped to tell you!"
¹⁶While he was still speaking, another messenger came and said, "The fire of God fell from the heavens and burned up the sheep and the servants, and I am the only one who has escaped to tell you!"
¹⁷While he was still speaking, another messenger came and said, "The Chaldeans formed three raiding parties and swept down on your camels and made off with them. They put the servants to the sword, and I am the only one who has escaped to tell you!"
¹⁸While he was still speaking, yet another messenger came and said, "Your sons and daughters were feasting and drinking wine at the oldest brother's house, ¹⁹when suddenly a mighty wind swept in from the desert and struck the four corners of the house. It collapsed on them and they are dead, and I am the only one who has escaped to tell you!"

> [20]At this, Job got up and tore his robe and shaved his head. Then he fell to the ground in worship [21]and said:
> "Naked I came from my mother's womb, and naked I will depart.
> The LORD gave and the LORD has taken away; may the name of the LORD be praised."
> [22]In all this, Job did not sin by charging God with wrongdoing. (Job 1:1-22, NIV)[5]

When I first preached this passage some years ago, we read the passage above just after our youth praise band had sung, "How He Loves Us"—that then-popular, contemporary Christian song made famous by the Dave Crowder Band:

> "And oh, how He loves us oh,
> Oh how He loves us, how He loves us oh...."[6]

What a contrast between the message of that song and the apparent message of this passage. "How He Loves Us"... and then the words we find here in Job? Are we talking about the same God here? What a difference between the God in song who "loves us so" and this seemingly capricious God of Job who seemingly wills or at least allows the worst to happen. What is going on? Well, that is exactly what we are here to find out.

Beginning at the End

In order to understand the opening chapters of this book, we need to know the whole story. Without knowing the whole story, we cannot make sense of the beginning.

---

[5] Unless otherwise indicated, all Scripture quotations come from *The Holy Bible, New International Version* (NIV). Biblica, 2011.
[6] David Crowder Band. "David Crowder*Band - How He Loves (Official Music Video)." *YouTube*, uploaded by davidcrowderband, 14 Oct. 2009, www.youtube.com/watch?v=TCunuL58odQ.

Have you ever watched one of your favorite television shows, and in the opening scene, the door of the apartment is just slightly ajar and the main character—the hero or star—is standing there over a dead body with a bloody knife in his/her hand with a stunned, shocked look on their face?

You know there must be more than meets the eye; there has to be some explanation for what you have just seen. There is no way—no way!—your favorite star or actor could have killed someone with the knife in hand, or at least there must be some terrific explanation. After the commercial break, the show resumes with "12 hours earlier..." at the bottom of the screen. We have to watch the whole show in order to make sense of the first five minutes.

The same is true of the book of Job—we can't read only the first chapter and say, "Ah! Wow! I've got it!" If we do, we presume a too simplistic plotline. We are reading Ancient Near Eastern literature—a somewhat deceptively complex literature with layers of meaning. So, how do we read this? We read this book, all of it, with the end in mind. So, let us get a preview of the whole story so we can come back to the beginning (spoiler alert!).

Job begins as a story of loss and pain. And, it only gets worse! After Job loses almost everything—his health included, three 'friends' come to bring him counsel, to help him through his pain and loss. Their worldview—and Job's as well—is one of "cause and effect," or as it often rendered with respect to Ancient Near Eastern thought, the "Retribution Principle" or karma: A general belief that doing good results in good, prosperity; doing bad results in bad, harm, illness.[7] To clarify—and this is crucial for our reading and understanding of Job—this worldview understood that the good

---

[7] "Major Background Issues from the Ancient Near East," *NIV Cultural Backgrounds Study Bible*. Craig S. Keener and John H. Walton, eds. (Grand Rapids, MI: Zondervan Publishers, 2016) *xxxv – xxxvii*.

and prosperity as well as the bad, harm, and illness all come from God (or the gods)—just dues for one's attitudes or behaviors.

Since this is how they see the world, the good friends who come to visit Job spend chapters trying to get him to admit he has some sin in his life—their message is, "You had to have done something bad, Job, or things would be going good for you." For them, nothing else serves to explain Job's losses and his suffering. Job gets frustrated with them, and they with him. Others show up to 'console' and advise Job.

Finally, in Job 38, God steps into the picture and shows Job that he—Job—really has no clue as to what is going on in the world, that his understanding of things is so shallow, so limited. In the end, God restores all of Job's fortunes and more besides, gives him a new family, and thus ends the book.

The very important thing to see in all of this is that at the beginning of this book Job is wrong. He is wrong about God. He is wrong about how the world works. He is wrong about himself. He is not evil or demonic or anti-God; he is simply wrong, mistaken—he does not yet understand how the world works, how God sees things. Job is mistaken ... something any of us could be at any time.

Have we not been mistaken at times in our lives? Have we not sworn something was so only to 'eat crow' later? We would not even have such a colorful saying—'eat crow'—if being mistaken and then coming to awareness were not a common thing. How many times have we been so sure that something was or happened a certain way in our families ... and then Mom pulls out the old photo album, and the evidence proves that we were wrong?

Well, just as we can be wrong, so can Job. And he is wrong in the beginning of the story. We need to keep that in mind as we go forward. We might be wrong, too, about the way we have seen the world or about how we have understood the workings of this world. Let us remain open to the possibilities.

Really, the structure of this story should not be a surprise to us. From ancient times to today, many stories begin with the main character in one place—geographically, emotionally, relationally, spiritually—and then he or she embarks on a journey of experiences, thought, or contemplation that leaves the character in a new place, with a new and greater understanding of self and/or the world. Just consider the *Epic of Gilgamesh* ... or Homer's *Iliad* and *Odyssey* ... or the Anglo-Saxon epic, *Beowulf*. In all of these and many others, the 'hero' of the story begins at one place and ends at a very different place.

This narrative structure holds true in much of biblical literature as well. Where is Moses at the beginning of his story? Unsure, untrusting, hesitant. Where is Moses at the end? Certain, faithful, bold. Where is Peter at the beginning of his story in the Gospels? He walks around braggadocios, usually with one if not both of his feet in his mouth. Where is Peter at Pentecost? A changed man with a new humility and greater understanding. Paul begins as Saul, a persecutor of the Church, and ends up penning half of the New Testament. Even the story of Jesus follows this structure: born a nobody in a manger ... then a teacher (rabbi) ... and finally the resurrected Savior of humankind. Talk about a reversal of fortune!

This is our story as well. We are not where we began. And if we are walking in the life of faith, we have an adventure before us that will take us where we cannot imagine. The changes that come with experiences, the reversals of thought—these can happen to any of us. In the same way, Job goes through a process of discovery and change.

Job at the beginning of this story—embracing the widely-held, common-yet-erroneous worldview of the times—is simply wrong in his understanding of God, the world, and how it all works.

Now that we know Job is just plain wrong, we can come back to the beginning and deal with what we find there.

God Challenged

In the opening part of Job 1, the "sons of God" have come before the LORD , and "the Adversary" (the Satan) is there as well. Who the "sons of God" are may be a fun question to pursue sometime (perhaps fodder for a master's thesis or a doctoral dissertation?), but we can presume that these beings are probably on God's side. Also, rather than dive into a prolonged discussion as to whether the Adversary and Satan and the Devil are all the same person or being, perhaps we can simply agree that these beings—whether one in the same or different creatures/forces—all of them run contrary to God and the things of God.

In this opening scene, the Adversary taunts God regarding Job saying that Job is faithful only because God is protecting and blessing him, that if God's protection and blessing were not there, Job would curse God (Job 1:9-11).

In short, this is the same as calling Job a "fair-weather friend," or, in this case, "fair-weather faithful"—like that person who praises God, goes to church, serves on committees, and smiles as long as all is well. Once some part of their life crashes, they disappear, they fall apart. They fall off the faith wagon. We have seen and known these folks (perhaps, we have even been that person somewhere along the way...?).

Ray,[8] a member of our high school youth group, was a good fellow. He was also living in a rough situation—a teenager in an unsupportive, single-parent home where money was scarce and affection all but unknown. When things were going well, he was right there at every Bible study, sitting on the second row in Sunday worship, smiling and greeting everyone. One day he simply was not there. We did not know that he had lost his job, but we knew something was up in his life because he had suddenly disappeared.

---

[8] Name changed.

He was happy and ready to praise God in the good times, but when life got out of control, he fled the church (just when he needed the church the most!).

Here in the story of Job, the Adversary is betting Job is fair-weather faithful and that if his world is somehow shaken, he will abandon God quickly and easily.

How is God to respond to this challenge? If God ignores or dismisses Satan and his accusations, it would be tantamount to admitting Satan is right—that Job is faithful only because all is well with him. So, what does God do?

> [12]The LORD said to Satan, "Very well, then, everything he has is in your power, but on the man himself do not lay a finger."
>
> Then Satan went out from the presence of the LORD.
>
> (Job 1:12)

First of all, going "out from the presence of the LORD" is never a good thing. It is to walk in darkness. It is to go in a way that God does not, to be where God is not. And, when we think of Satan, this is exactly what we expect—the Adversary, the Satan, is one who operates outside the will and reign of God.

Then—and this is very important—we need to see who is doing what in the life of Job. "…Everything he has is in your power…." Who is the cause of the Sabean raid? Who is the source of the devouring fire? (The servant says 'fire of God,' but he's living in the same erroneous worldview as Job and his friends, thinking everything good and bad is from God.) Who is the source of the Chaldean attack? Who is the source of the desert winds? Not God. Satan is the one who brings all of these calamities to bear on Job. Therefore, a better, truer utterance on the part of Job in his situation would have been this:

The LORD gave and Satan (the Adversary) has taken away….

Interestingly, this is not the only occasion in which God and Satan have this sort of conversation. Evidently, Satan is astounded again and again that people would actually love God and want to serve God. So, Satan seems to want to prove this to himself from time to time by testing God's people.

In the Gospel of Luke in the New Testament, we find Jesus speaking to his disciples just before his crucifixion, just before they arrive at the garden of Gethsemane for that agonizing time of prayer. Jesus says, "Simon, Simon, Satan has asked to sift all of you as wheat. But I have prayed for you, Simon, that your faith may not fail. And when you have turned back, strengthen your brothers" (Luke 22:31).

So, here again, Satan comes before God and asks to test the faith of God's people.

When I went back and read this first chapter of Job again, and as I re-read this passage in Luke, I kept asking, Why? Why would God allow Satan to do this? What is going on?

Many theologians and pastors have attempted to explain or justify suffering by claiming that suffering is the means by which God disciplines and/or teaches us. Okay. That may be so. There may be times that God disciplines us for our errors or teaches us some lesson.[9] Yet, these situations we see here in Scripture—in Job and Luke—do not seem to be times in which God is somehow 'disciplining' the faithful for unfaithfulness or teaching the faithful an important lesson. So, what is going on?

Perhaps you saw it before I did. As I read and reread the words of Job 1 and Luke 22, the answer hit me quite suddenly. I am not talking about some idea that popped into my head; I am not talking about some clever re-reading of Scripture to fit my own preconceptions. The truth is right there in black-and-white (or red, if you have a red-letter Bible) in those last words of Jesus on this

---

[9] See Hebrews 12:4-11.

topic in Luke 22: "And when you have turned back, strengthen your brothers...." Not "if" you turn back, but "when" you turn back. What does this mean?

You see, we talk a lot about trusting in God, of having faith in God—and rightfully so. We desperately need to learn to trust, to place our faith and confidence in God. However, one of the things the book of Job teaches us, and that Jesus shows us in Luke, is that God has faith in us. God was so confident—trusting, believing—in Job's faithfulness that God could allow Satan to do his foolishness ... and God was certain that Job's faith would not fail—regardless of the circumstances of life. Jesus was so confident in the faithfulness of his band of disciples that he could allow Satan to "sift them as wheat" knowing they would remain faithful. In the same way, God has faith in us—in you, in me.

Let that sink in: God...has...faith...in...US!

What we see here is a confidence that God has in God's people. God believes that we believe. God trusts that we trust. God is confident of our love. God is confident that we will not let go of our faith regardless of the circumstances in life. In spite of the storms of life, in spite of the loss and hurt and pain ... in spite of the 'sifting' that may come our way in the form of suffering. God believes, trusts, has faith that we will remain faithful. And, if we were to wander, to walk away for even a season, God maintains an unwavering hope in our return.

Wow! That, in the words of a dear friend of mine, is 'crazy-amazing.' We need not wonder then at all why Paul would pen those foundational words some two thousand years or more after Job—words that describe the foundation of our lives because they are the foundation of God's view and attitude towards us:

> And now these three remain: faith, hope and love.
> (I Cor. 13:13)

Faith, hope, and love sustain us because they reflect God's way towards us—God has faith in our faithfulness, hope for our righteousness, and love unconditional for us. We are to respond in kind—we are to trust, have confidence in, believe in God's goodness; we are hope—to look forward to whatever 'better' that God is bringing to pass; and, we are to love—to act selflessly towards all, towards God and neighbor.

Job proves God right. Even though Job was wrong in his understanding of God (presuming God was the cause of his suffering), he was and remained confident in God. Even though his worldview was simplistic and incomplete, his simple faith in God—in the goodness, rightness, and trustworthiness of God—remained true and sure.

On the Journey through Suffering—

Perhaps some who are reading here have made that same leap that Job made, mistakenly believing that everything that happens is from God. Job teaches us—better, reminds us—that there is an 'adversarial' power (or powers) that wants to see us fall and fail. In this narrative, the Adversary, Satan, is the one who takes, divides, destroys, and kills. We presume this same evil, contrary-to-God power remains active in the world around us today in some way robbing us of health, happiness, and wholeness.

When I first wrote these words, the COVID-19 pandemic had most of the world locked in homes, many people out of work, and far too many frightened. Over half a million people had died in the US alone. The economic fallout had already been devastating to large and small businesses alike. And, I had already heard some say, "This is God punishing us for our sins."

Late one afternoon, as Marjan and I talked, she expressed her understandable frustration with her own situation: "If there is a God and he is good, why would he do this to me? I'm not a bad person. And if God is good as you say, why doesn't he heal me?"

Real questions from a real person facing real suffering.

I told her that I did not believe that her cancer was from God. And about the healing? God sometimes heals in 'supernatural' or miraculous ways, but more often God works through the hands, words, and compassion of amazing health-care providers and workers. I do not think Marjan's cancer is sent by Satan—there are other sources of suffering besides the evil forces we find in this passage of Job, but more on that later.

Evil, contrary-to-God powers do bring about some of the suffering we see robbing people of the gift of life that God has given. Destructive powers wreak havoc on the world. I may not go so far as to say that the COVID virus is a demonic force, but I will say that this virus (and cancer and any other illness) has an effect on humans that is in direct opposition to the will of God. God's will includes wholeness, joy, and peace.

We find in Job and in the Gospels that the same God—in whom we trust, in whom we place our faith, to whom we lift our prayers and praise — the same God of creation and history has faith in us, trusts us to remain faithful, or to return if we wander, no matter what we go through.

Therefore, how shall we now live knowing that the God of the universe, the Creator, has faith in us, that the Creator has confidence in us? How do we need to alter our worldview? What have we been seeing wrongly? Have we been right there with Job, blaming God for all of the bad stuff in our lives?

When we encounter the trials and pains and hurts of this life, let us not make the mistake of Job and think God is the cause of our suffering. Let us claim the truths we find in Scripture that God is on our side, that God is the author of all goodness and blessing. But, more on this in the chapters to come.

And to think we have made it only into Job chapter 1. What else awaits us in this journey? On we go....

Questions for Reflection—

1. Have you thought that everything in life is from God—the good and the bad?

_____
_____
_____

2. What are some of the difficulties or sufferings that you have blamed on God?

_____
_____
_____

3. How might things have played out differently if you realized that God was not working against you?

_____
_____
_____

Chapter 3
"YOU GIVE AND TAKE AWAY"
JOB 1:21

"Naked I came from my mother's womb,
and naked I will depart.
The LORD gave and the LORD has taken away;
may the name of the LORD be praised."

Songs get stuck in my head. Does that happen to you? Many times, it is not even a song that I really like or love, but the tune is catchy—and there it is, bouncing around inside my head all day long. Usually, I think that if I just listen to the song really loud, I can quell the tune in my brain. Sometimes that works. Sometimes it does not.

"Blessed Be Your Name," by Matt Redman, is one such song.[10] Overall, the lyrics are good, the theology sound. No matter what is going on in life, we praise God. Whether we are in "the land that is plentiful" or if we are "found in the desert place"—no matter what, no matter our circumstances, we bless and praise God. We find that same idea in the Psalms and in other Scriptures as well.

But, then we get to that piece of the refrain, and the beauty and theology of this song all fall apart (sorry, Matt):

---

[10] Redmond, Matt. "Blessed Be Your Name." YouTube. https://www.youtube.com/watch?v=du0il6d-DAk.

> You give and take away
> You give and take away
> My heart will choose to say
> Lord blessed be Your name.

And these lines of 'bad theology' come right out of the mouth of Job.

Sovereignty ≠ Universal Cause

One of the key doctrines or teachings of the Scriptures that the Church affirms is the "sovereignty of God." 'Sovereign' means "possessing...supreme power" or exercising "supreme authority." [11] We talk about our God as "omnipotent" or all-powerful. This claim grows out of the understanding of Creation as set forth in Genesis—everything that is, exists because God spoke it into being. When we read the Revelation of John, we find that God gets the last word at the end of time as well.

All through Scripture, we find the sovereignty of God affirmed beginning in the book of Genesis where God is called "El Shaddai"—a phrase often translated in our English translations as "God Almighty" (cf. Gen. 17:1; 28:3; 35:11; 43:14; 48:3). The power and might of God come through Scriptures all the time.

In Jeremiah 32:17, we find "Ah, Sovereign LORD, you have made the heavens and the earth by your great power and outstretched arm. Nothing is too hard for you." The Psalmist echoes this same idea in Psalm 135:6: "The LORD does whatever pleases him, in the heavens and on the earth, in the seas and all their depths."

---

[11] "Sovereign." *Merriam-Webster.com Dictionary*, Merriam-Webster, https://www.merriam-webster.com/dictionary/sovereign. Accessed 10 May. 2021.

This truth shows up in the New Testament in the mouth of Jesus in Matthew 19:26—"Jesus looked at them and said, 'With man this is impossible, but with God all things are possible'" (see also Mark 10:27; Luke 18:27; Luke 1:37).

The sovereignty of God is not to be doubted. Many Christians around the world affirm God's sovereignty in the Apostles' Creed each Sunday: "I believe in God the Father Almighty, Maker of Heaven and Earth…." We claim and hold on to this truth of God's sovereignty, and we rightfully find a great deal of assurance and security in such a statement. However, many—like Job—then tend to make a great leap of logic, and when they do, they go wrong. They go wrong and they step outside biblical doctrine. The leap of logic goes like this:

If God is all-powerful, if God is omnipotent, then God must control or cause everything that happens in this world. That is, everything that happens is because our omnipotent, almighty, all-powerful God is making it happen.

We see this in the common social media posts about how "…Everything happens for a reason." The implication is that God is behind it all, God is the 'reason' for everything that happens.

In order to uphold this worldview, people have even created new theologies to support it, theologies that we hear in statements like these:

"Ah! I didn't get that job that I really wanted because God has something better for me."

"Oh, yes, the car broke down—God was saving us from an accident down the road."

"Well, that relationship didn't work out because God has a better person for me."

These statements and so many like them—that I hear far too often—are an attempt to reconcile a belief in a sovereign God who is the cause of everything that happens with regard to the unpleasant (or horrific) circumstances of our lives. But, we run into two problems with this worldview, with this theology.

First of all, this worldview is not biblical. The idea that God is the cause of everything that happens is not a biblical worldview or theology. When we scour the breadth and depth of Scripture, we do not find a single instance—not in any narrative, description, nor conversation—wherein God brings about failure, broken relationships, harm, sickness, or anything else and then suggests, "…Because I have something better for you."

We do see pain and suffering and loss fall on people in the Scriptures, but not because God has something better waiting down the road. Sometimes people may suffer loss or pain as a part of discipline or correction as we have already mentioned or as a result of bad choices or evil actions, but not because God has something better waiting. God may have better things waiting for us in the future, but God does not wound and harm us as prelude to blessing. This is a false worldview, or at least a non-biblical if not anti-biblical worldview. God simply does not work that way in Scripture.

In one of the starkest examples from Scripture, Jesus has the perfect opportunity to employ or affirm this erroneous theology in his discourse in Luke 13 discussing some people who were killed by Pilate and eighteen others who died in the collapse of a tower.

> Now there were some present at that time who told Jesus about the Galileans whose blood Pilate had mixed with their sacrifices. Jesus answered, "Do you think that these Galileans were worse sinners than all the other Galileans because they suffered this way? I tell you, no! But unless you repent, you too will all perish. Or those eighteen who died when the tower in Siloam fell on

them—do you think they were more guilty than all the others living in Jerusalem? I tell you, no! But unless you repent, you too will all perish." (Luke 13:1-5)

Jesus has the perfect opportunity here to put these deaths on God, but he very clearly and intentionally does not put these horrors on God. Pilate did this. The tower fell. These things happened to these people, yes, but not because they were evil or any worse than anyone else—Jesus is very clear about that.

This worldview or belief that our Sovereign God causes everything that happens translates into the things we say (and believe!) with regard to our lives and the lives of others. This way of thinking includes not only those times people say, "I guess God didn't want me to have that job," but also finds its way into broader issues regarding climate—"God must be punishing us—this drought is terrible" or "I don't understand why God is sending this hurricane…"—all the way to, "God sent COVID to call us repentance."

This presumption or worldview, my friends, that all things are caused by God is not only a false assumption, but also a dangerous assumption—giving us a diabolically skewed worldview. And, it is the assumption (false assumption!) Job, and later his friends, makes here at the beginning of this narrative.

"The LORD gave and the LORD has taken away; may the name of the LORD be praised." (Job 1:21b)

At best, Job is half right in this declaration. Yet, I have heard Christians quote this bit of Job's skewed thinking so many times presuming it to be true.

Another of the contemporary songs that perhaps most poignantly captures this worldview is "Thy Will" by Hillary Scott & the Scott Family. Ms. Scott's voice is beautiful, enchanting; however, the lyrics reveal this mistaken view of reality, something contrary to a biblical worldview. The lyrics include these lines:

> I may never understand
> That my broken heart is a part of your plan

And later in the song:

> I know you're good
> But this don't feel good right now

These lyrics claim that God is the source of the speaker's/singer's broken heart, that our good God brings not only 'not good' things our way but also bad, painful, hurtful things as well. God is omnipotent and all-causing in the lyrics of this song.[12]

Perhaps some people really do find consolation in ascribing everything to God. That does not work for me and many others. To consider that God gave my father fatal cancer when he was only 50 years old does not console me nor does it bring me joyfully to God's throne. In fact, when my father died when I was a rising senior in high school, I decided that I wanted nothing to do with such a God—if God was indeed the cause of my father's death. For a season, I rejected the Christian faith and searched for purpose and peace elsewhere.

Ascribing everything to God is wrong—biblically wrong; simply incorrect. To believe everything is from God is to embrace a lie. And, as Leslie Weatherhead points out in that wonderful little volume, *The Will of God*, if we console someone with a lie, in the end there is no real consolation.[13]

---

[12] How I wish well-meaning, well-intentioned songwriters would find a theologian or Bible scholar to run their lyrics by before letting loose their catchy, stick-in-the-mind songs.
[13] Weatherhead, Leslie D. *The Will of God*. New York: Abingdon-Cokesbury Press, 1944, p.16.

Perhaps somewhere along the way you, as I, may have said these words—with the very best intentions—to those you have known, hoping to provide a bit of comfort to someone in a time of loss: "God is in control; the Lord gives and the Lord takes away." How many times I have stood with family members and loved ones at a funeral service or in the 'receiving line' at the funeral home and heard these kinds of words:

"God always takes the good ones."

"I guess God needed her more than we do."

"We all know, the Lord gives, and the Lord takes away."

Many people seek consolation in thoughts like this, finding some kind of peace in assigning even the most horrific things to God.

Today (if the situation were appropriate for a teaching moment), I would stop the person then and there and say, "Do you really think God gave this woman cancer?" "Do you think this young man was taken by God? I thought it was the fool driving drunk?" "Do you really believe God willed and wanted this grandmother to be taken by COVID?"

The Problem of Evil

Let us get back to this issue of the 'sovereignty of God.' We like the idea (sometimes) of our omnipotent, all-powerful, all-in-control God directing all the happenings of our lives. But, there are problems with that approach to life, to seeing things this way.

If God is so completely sovereign that everything happens at God's bidding and desire, how does that allow for or account for the existence of evil, the evil one, Satan, the Devil? If everything is from God—the good and the bad—then "evil" has no need to exist, or evil is just a term we use for those acts of God we do not like. Right? If God truly controls/causes everything, then there really is no devil or evil force in the world. If there is no real evil, what we call "evil" is just God acting in a way contrary to our will or understanding.

Yet, when we take the greater world of Scripture into account, we know that this is simply *not* true—evil and evil powers do exist. Jesus wrestles with the devil in the Gospels in his wilderness temptation (Matthew 4:1ff, Mark 1:12ff, Luke 4:1ff). Paul writes about Satan and the devil ... about "powers of this dark world" and "spiritual forces of evil" (Ephesians 6:12). Also, all we have to do is look at that important prayer that Jesus taught his disciples, that many Christians around the world recite Sunday after Sunday: "...But deliver us from evil..." (Matt. 6:13). In some translations, we find "deliver us from the evil one"—but the idea of evil is clearly stated in Jesus' prayer. Evil and evil forces exist. So, if evil exists and impacts our lives, what about the sovereignty of God?

Some of my students and colleagues at a seminary where I taught for a season would be quick to argue that "God simply 'allows'—in God's omniscience and wisdom—the evil to reign briefly in our lives in order to teach us or discipline us."

Let us bring that idea back to our reading in Job. In this understanding (allowing for teaching or discipline), God basically steps back and allows the Satan to abuse Job, to rob him of family, health, and wealth—but would this be to teach Job or to discipline him? In Job 1:8, God declares that Job is "blameless and upright." So, God allows this to happen in order to teach Job what? In order to discipline him for what reason?

In fact, as we go to the text, we find—not suggested but stated—that God neither teaching nor disciplining; rather, God is allowing the Satan to prove to himself if Job is truly faithful to God or if Job is only situationally faithful.

That seems rather capricious of God. And God certainly did not consult with Job to see if this would be okay or not.

Some may be tempted to hit the brakes here and ask me, "Who are you to question God?" Others will talk about the "mystery" of God—God does things we cannot understand. If I am questioning God (and I am), then I am joining a host of biblical examples in questioning God, so I gladly join their ranks—Abraham, Moses, David ... and most of the prophets! If there is a mystery here, then you and I will not solve it. But, what if there is a clear and obvious answer?

A Possibility...

So, God is capricious in the story of Job and in our lives, too, or perhaps something else is true, perhaps something else is going on in this text and in our own reality. What if this is what is happening—

What if God—the all-powerful, omnipotent One—voluntarily limits God's own sovereignty.

Does that sound crazy? If it does, you may have missed a very important part of the Christian message:

In your relationships with one another, have the same mindset as Christ Jesus:

> Who, being in very nature God,
>   did not consider equality with God something to be
> used to his own advantage;
> rather, he made himself nothing
>   by taking the very nature of a servant,
>   being made in human likeness.
> And being found in appearance as a man,
>   he humbled himself
>   by becoming obedient to death—
>   even death on a cross!   (Philippians 2:5-8)

So, God does voluntarily limit God's own sovereignty. That is, God, the omni-Everything, chooses not to be omni-Everything (when One is omni-Everything, One can certainly decide not to be omni-Everything or decide not to play the "omni" card.)

Certainly, in the life of Jesus, God in the flesh, we see that evil affects, impacts his life. The powers of evil work against Jesus' life and ministry, and the evil or ignorant decisions of people around him seriously affect his life—even lead to his death. He doesn't play the 'Divine' card to save himself, and God the Father doesn't descend with that army of angels. We can safely presume that God can limit God's own sovereignty.

So, for the next few chapters of this book, let us hold this reality in our minds the idea, that God steps back while another force reigns in Job's reality, a force that is evil, hurtful, destructive. Let us see how this plays out if we look at Job's situation from that perspective—a perspective from which we could view our own lives.

Free-Will

Both God's willingness to step back and the powers-of-evil's harmful actions indicate something of them that is also true of us—"free-will." In addition to evil forces in the world that attack, harm, or derail us, God—the sovereign, omnipotent, all-powerful God—has given us "free-will": the ability to choose, to make choices that are for or against this same God.

Even though Christians through the ages have debated understandings of "free-will," Scripture clearly affirms our ability to choose with regard to many aspects of our lives:

> "You are free to eat from any tree in the garden; but you must not eat from the tree of the knowledge of good and evil..." (Genesis 2:16b-17a)

"...choose for yourselves this day whom you will serve...." (Joshua 24:15)

"Come to me, all you who are weary...." (Matthew 11:28)

"Whoever wants to be my disciple must deny themselves and take up their cross daily and follow me." (Luke 9:23)

These important passages and so many more indicate that we have to make choices in life, important choices, ultimate choices. We humans participate in the story that God is unfolding through time and space. Our participation begins in the Garden of Eden. There, Adam and Eve commit the first sin resulting in the first suffering (see Genesis 3), and their sin results in a broken world. Their act of free-will results in pain, suffering, hurt, illness, and death ...for them and for every generation that has followed. Talk about the power of our decisions to impact the lives of others! We suffer today in a broken world because of Adam and Eve's choices. Our choices, the choices of those around us, and the choices of people in history impact our lives and the lives of others.

Adam and Eve disobeyed God due to fear, arrogance, or egotism, and the whole world suffers the effects—sickness, pain, division, and death.[14]

Our European ancestors in North America determined that enslaving others and forcing them to work would be the best way to build their economy, and millions suffer today after three centuries of systemic racism.

---

[14] For a thorough discussion of the original sin and the effects of sin, see Jon A. Herrin. *Making Sense of It All: Reflections on the Ancient Narratives of Genesis.* KDP Publishing, 2020, and *Genesis for Today: Redeeming Ancient Narratives for Contemporary Living*, KDP Publishing, 2023.

Society decides that fossil fuels serve as the best way to drive their economy, and the fall-out from drilling, fracking, transporting, and burning those fuels impacts eco-systems, climate, and human health for generations. People, animals, and the land suffer.

A company executive decides he can make millions by secretly skimming the retirement accounts of unsuspecting employees. He takes millions and runs, and thousands suffer the loss of their retirement savings.

A man drinks too much and decides that he can drive. He gets in his car, drives too fast, runs a red light, and kills an innocent driver in another car. Families suffer for years to come.

We can choose to care for our bodies, eat well, exercise, and get plenty of rest; we can ignore science and fill our bodies with poisonous foods and waste our lives as couch potatoes in front of the television. If we live this way and become sick because of it, we suffer.[15]

Our decisions—our acts of free-will—can cause suffering in our own lives and in the lives of others. Some of those decisions are willful, knowing decisions—we know that our decisions will cause suffering. Some of those decisions are made in ignorance—but that does not lessen the resulting suffering for us or others.

On the Journey through Suffering—

The Adversary and powers of evil can act against us, we can act against God, we can act selfishly or even foolishly and ignorantly ... and the results are not God's will or God's doing.

---

[15] Some people who do "everything right" also become ill or die. We must remember, as stated above, that we live in a world broken by sin. Bad, painful, destructive things will happen, no matter what, in our broken world.

Before my friend, Marjan, had her world rocked by cancer, suffering had already come to her life.

When she still lived in Iran, she met and fellow in love with a fellow—an Iranian living in the U.S. But, there was a hitch. In Iran, people must register their chosen or family religion. While Marjan was practically an agnostic or atheist, she was registered at a Muslim. The man she fell in love with was registered as a Christian. In Iran, marrying someone for a different religion is illegal.

Marjan and her fiancé met up in the country of Georgia (in Eastern Europe on the Black Sea) where they were allowed to marry. Getting Marjan to the US took another two years of paperwork and interviews. Finally, she arrived in California to begin living her "happily ever after."

Shortly after arriving in the US, she discovered that her new husband was bipolar, and he wasn't too keen on taking his medication. While not physically abusive, he was verbally abusive and lazy (what a great Christian witness!). Marjan tried everything to make it work. In the end, he asked for a divorce. When he left her, he told her that their house would be repossessed by the bank in 20 days, that she should find another place to live.

After the divorce, she discovered that her ex-husband had taken out credit cards in her name. She was left with no income, no home, and over $4000 in credit card debt. And, she spoke little English.

She got the only job she could find—food delivery. And she began living out of her car until she had enough saved to get an apartment.

Marjan understands as well as any of us how someone else's actions can lead to our suffering. She understands how broken people can break our lives. She understands that we can suffer even when we have done all we can to do that is right.

We must understand that in this world there are evil forces arrayed against us, and we have the autonomy to make mistakes, to act contrary to God's will, to do damage to ourselves and to others. As Christians, we recognize that Adam and Eve's decision forever impacted humanity—we now live in a broken world, a brokenness that my friend Marjan is, unfortunately, well acquainted with. God is not the source or cause of suffering brought about by these events in our lives. COVID, cancer, lost jobs, hurricanes, car problems, relationship troubles—these are not the work of God. We live in a broken world filled with broken people who act out of their brokenness. No wonder we and all the world around us experience suffering. In fact, it is a wonder that we do not experience *more* suffering!

If we can grasp these ideas, we can then realize that Job the man is simply (tragically!) mistaken in thinking that God is doing to him what he is experiencing. When we read the passage carefully and closely, we see what is really going on here, and we see who is giving and who is taking away.

Questions for Reflection—

1. How have you suffered for your own bad decisions?

_____

_____

_____

2. How have you suffered because of others' bad decisions?

_____

_____

_____

3. Have you seen suffering in this world that was the result of evil?
_____
_____
_____

Chapter 4
BEING A FRIEND
JOB 2:1-13

God is not the seemingly capricious Being people have often (unintentionally) read into Job 1 and into their own reality, and God is not the cause of all our pain and suffering. Job has taught us or reminded us that other forces are at work in this world that are contrary to God and God's wishes for us. Those forces include (but are not limited to) Satan—the Accuser, the Devil, demons, and "rulers...authorities...powers of this dark world and...spiritual forces of evil in the heavenly realms" (Ephesians 6:12). We rediscover that human free-will has broken our world and our lives, and our own free-will decisions can cause suffering in our lives and the lives of others. We must recognize and realize that the 'bad' in our lives does not come from God.

Back to the Story...

After Job is stripped of family, livestock, and crops, Job remains faithful, remains confident in his God. He does not curse God. He accepts what comes his way. We do not have all of the details—he may have gone home and kicked the cat, but he does not rail against the Creator or shake a fist at the heavens. While he considers God the cause of the situation in which he finds himself, he does not curse God. We have much to learn from this man.

While Job suffers unimaginable loss, he does not cave, he does not turn his back on God. Things did not go as the Adversary, Satan, had anticipated. And, though Satan is disappointed, he is not giving up the fight. In Job 2, Satan returns to God with a new plan.

> ³Then the LORD said to Satan, "…[Job] still maintains his integrity, though you incited me against him to ruin him without any reason."
>
> ⁴"Skin for skin!" Satan replied. "A man will give all he has for his own life. ⁵But now stretch out your hand and strike his flesh and bones, and he will surely curse you to your face."
>
> ⁶The LORD said to Satan, "Very well, then, he is in your hands; but you must spare his life."
>
> ⁷So Satan went out from the presence of the LORD and afflicted Job with painful sores from the soles of his feet to the crown of his head.   (Job 2:3-7)

Satan decides that this action—robbing Job of his health—will surely drive Job away from God. Yes, this, too, is Satan's doing, not God's. We clearly see the source of Job's suffering right there in v.7. If there was any doubt before, the text here puts all uncertainties to rest: "So, Satan … afflicted Job with painful sores…." Satan; not God. We know where this illness and suffering come from—and they do not come from God. They are not "God's will." They are not "part of God's plan."

Satan thinks that if Job loses his health, that will do it—Job's faith and trust in God will crumble! Our health is indeed a precious thing.

My wife, Jeanne, suffers as I write this chapter. One evening recently, my wife realized she had not plugged in her phone to charge. The lights in the living room were already off since we were preparing for bed, so—as we all do from time to time—she trusted herself to navigate the living area to get to the phone plug. Just before getting to her destination, a corner jumped in front of her, and she slammed her foot into the piece of wall leaving her with a sprained middle toe. The following morning, that toe was blue from just before the toenail and back about an inch or more. While she walked ever so gingerly for days after, she walked a bit better after we taped that blue toe to one of the neighboring toes.

That little, middle toe does practically nothing for Jeanne day after day. Once sprained, it affected her walking, her sitting, and her sleeping. Yes, our health is precious to us. A small sprain, a head-cold, a bruise—any of these small things can knock us out of whack. Even a pimple can ruin our day—just ask a teenager (or an adult!). Or course, more serious illnesses and conditions certainly impact our lives … and in this passage, we see that Satan is banking on such an illness to impact even one's faith.

Job has more than a sprain or a pain, more than a cold or flu, and more than a pimple. Poor Job has "painful sores from the soles of his feet to the crown of his head." And, they seem to be either puss-filled or runny—he scrapes the sores with a shard of pottery (2:8). He is miserable. And, he looks terrible. In fact, his wife probably wonders if all this 'bad luck' is catchy. Job is not ready to turn his back on God, but his wife is:

> ⁹His wife said to him, "Are you still maintaining your integrity? Curse God and die!"   (Job 2:9)

Enough already! Can't you see that God has abandoned you? Just get it over with!

Job is not ready to throw in the towel just yet. We do not know how old Job is, but he is old enough to have had grown children and to have amassed significant possessions. If the earliest dates of Job are correct (placing him in the Patriarchal period—around 2000BC), then the average life expectancy for people in Job's world is about 20 years. [16]

Considering the wealth he has amassed and his family size, we can presume that he has beaten the odds and might even have made into his 40's—an 'old man' for his time period. And, having lived to this 'ripe, old age,' we can imagine that he has walked with God for quite a while.

I can imagine Job talking to God as he walks the fields checking on his herds. I can imagine him out under the stars at night in prayer. God seems to have been a significant part of his life for quite a while. Job is not giving up yet. So, he responds to his wife:

> [10]He replied, "You are talking like a foolish woman. Shall we accept good from God, and not trouble?" (Job 2:10)

Two things come through loud and clear in this passage.

First, Job definitely believes that God causes all things to happen; Job thinks God is author of good and bad. This we already knew about Job. The second thing is that the faith of Job shines here in an amazing way—he earnestly believes that all that is happening to him is from God, yet he remains faithful. This reveals a confidence, a faith, that is quite beyond me—perhaps beyond many of us.

In Job's mind, God robs him of his sons and daughters; God robs him of his honestly earned possessions; God robs him of his health—and he is to remain faithful still? Though his theology and worldview are flawed (for the time being), his faith and his trust in

---

[16] For an introduction to the debate regarding 'life expectancy' vs. 'lifespan', begin with this article: Radford, Benjamin. "Human Lifespans Nearly Constant for 2,000 Years." *Livescience.Com*, 21 Aug. 2009, www.livescience.com/10569-human-lifespans-constant-2-000-years.html.

God are real and powerful. I mean, to believe that the horrors of one's life are from God and still remain faithful to that God? That is trust!

When I was sixteen years old, I came home from my after-school job one August afternoon to hear the news that my dad had been diagnosed with advanced cancer of the intestines, stomach, and liver. A miracle was the only thing that would bring him through. Since my dad was both a minister and a missionary, a good man, a man who had brought hundreds if not thousands to faith, surely the God he served would undo this horrible wrong. In May of the following year, my dad died. I was furious at God. I was so angry and disillusioned that I turned my back on God. In effect, I decided to "curse God" and find something more trustworthy, if it were to be found.

Thankfully, though my search took me far and wide, I found my way back to God—but with a new and deeper understanding. I now wonder if Job did not take a similar journey that simply was not recorded. Does he arrive at the end of this journey with new understanding of God and the world? Let us press on and see.

Three Friends

Job's three friends arrive—

> [11] When Job's three friends, Eliphaz the Temanite, Bildad the Shuhite and Zophar the Naamathite, heard about all the troubles that had come upon him, they set out from their homes and met together by agreement to go and sympathize with him and comfort him. [12] When they saw him from a distance, they could hardly recognize him; they began to weep aloud, and they tore their robes and sprinkled dust on their heads. [13] Then they sat on the ground with him for seven days and seven

> nights. No one said a word to him, because they saw how great his suffering was.   (Job 2:11-13)

The three friends come and sit with Job, sit in silence. They hurt with him, they suffer with him for seven days. This is good. This is what friends do. Friends come in the moment of need, they come alongside us in the midst of pain, and they hurt with us. In some of the hardest moments of my life, it was so important to have someone sit with me.

Tommy, my best friend in high school, sat with me (or allowed me to sit with him) so often through my father's illness and death and the weeks and months after. Teri sat with me and visited me when I was in the hospital during a dark season in college. Fr. Gary was there for me during graduate school as I adjusted to being a newlywed and as I struggled with the angst of self-understanding. Mom and Papa were there with me for my wife's C-Section when our first child, Jesse Elizabeth, came into the world and through the stresses of that time. And, of course, my infinitely patient wife, Jeanne, has been with me through more of these kinds of times than I can even remember.

Yes, for their arrival and their sitting with their friend, the three friends of Job must be admired.

But, they open their mouths, speak—and it all falls apart.

They (with best intentions, I'm sure) begin to offer advice, advice that is based on their faulty, cause-and-effect theology, their "retribution principle" worldview, a theology and worldview that says that God rewards good and punishes bad (which God does, but not in the simplistic, cause-effect manner Job and his friends presume).

We see this way of thinking in Eliphaz' first response:

> [8]As I have observed, those who plow evil
> and those who sow trouble reap it.

> ⁹At the breath of God they perish;
>> at the blast of his anger they are no more.
>>> (Job 4:8-9)

Bildad has this same worldview—a worldview that suggests that sin incurs destruction and pain, that if Job would just live right and get things together in his life, then all would be well:

> ³Does God pervert justice?
>> Does the Almighty pervert what is right?
> ⁴When your children sinned against him,
>> he gave them over to the penalty of their sin.
> ⁵But if you will seek God earnestly
>> and plead with the Almighty,
> ⁶if you are pure and upright,
>> even now he will rouse himself on your behalf
>> and restore you to your prosperous state.
>>> (Job 8:3-6)

So, suffering in the penalty of sin? Then, how do we account for the many Christians—faithful people—who have been martyred through the centuries? Was that a result of sin? How many Christians were fed to the lions in Rome? How many "pure and upright" Christians have suffered or been killed by violence—precisely because of their faithfulness—or by illness? We might as what alternate reality do these "friends" live in?

And, finally Zophar weighs in—he, too, is convinced that all that has come upon Job is the result of sin. Somewhere along the way, Job has messed up and all he needs to do is renounce his sin and turn back to God:

> ¹³"Yet if you devote your heart to him
>> and stretch out your hands to him,
> ¹⁴if you put away the sin that is in your hand
>> and allow no evil to dwell in your tent,
> ¹⁵then, free of fault, you will lift up your face;

> you will stand firm and without fear.
> ¹⁶You will surely forget your trouble,
>   recalling it only as waters gone by.
> ¹⁷Life will be brighter than noonday,
>   and darkness will become like morning.
>
> (Job 11:13-17)

If we are suffering—according to the theology and worldview of these friends—then it is because of sin in our lives and this is exactly what they tell Job. However, we have already seen clearly in Job 1 and 2 that the suffering in Job's life is not from God but from the Adversary. Besides that, we have heard God clearly declare Job's blamelessness and uprightness. Yet, these friends cling to their worldview and would agree whole-heartedly with Job's declaration in Job 1: The LORD gives and the LORD takes away – the LORD has given what you had and taken it all away.

How do we apply such a worldview, such an understanding, to the seven-year-old girl at my friends' church who was out running, playing, and laughing at VBS one week … and two weeks later died of an amazingly aggressive disease? How do we say such words to the parents whose child is suddenly snatched by an alligator at Disney World? How can we utter such words to the families of police officers who are cut down in life of duty during a moment of madness? How do we quote these words to the family whose son, brother, or father took his own life? Do we share these words with the people of Puerto Rico, Florida, and the Carolinas who deal with the aftermath of hurricane destruction? How do we say these words to the Guatemalan woman who has risked everything with her children to come to America only to have her children ripped from her arms at the US border and placed in custody? Really? The LORD did all of these things? The LORD God, the Author of life, the Creator, caused or committed these horrific acts? Are we ready to say all of these events and happenings are simply and uniquely the result of the sin of those who suffer the loss or pain?

Blame disease, blame inadequate signage, blame an unbalanced man with a gun, blame mental illness, blame unjust laws and short-sighted politicians, blame the brokenness of our world, blame the selfishness and short-sightedness of others, blame the Adversary ... but we must stop blaming God for the pain and suffering of this world!

Turning Things Around

These well-meaning friends talk to Job about God. They share all of their so-called wisdom and insight. But, I wonder, do they ever get around to talking *to God about Job*?

We who have found our hope and foundation in God want others to find what we have found. Many of us are almost desperate that others come to faith in God. With the best intentions, we may be so quick to talk to others about God. We are so driven to help others find what we have found in God through Jesus. Some even live in danger of becoming that caricature—the 'Bible-thumping witness.' Yes, we do want to share with others about God, but we often forget to talk to God about those who do not yet know God ... or who are suffering and most desperately need God's help in their lives.

During the early 2000's, I served a north Georgia congregation made up of wonderfully diverse folks who wanted to engage in different kinds of ministries. One of our passionate laypersons got connected with prison ministries, and soon we had a team ready to go and visit an Atlanta-area prison. We completed the training that enabled us to clearly and concisely 'share the faith,' we were handed tracts to leave with inmates, and off we went.

I had two experiences in the prison. One was in the open bunk area where 50+ inmates would hang out and sleep. I began talking to one fellow and in short order, there were about 10 guys gathered around as I talked about the passage of Scripture where Jesus tells the story of the shepherd who leaves the 99 sheep to find the missing one (Luke 15:3-7). I wanted them to know they were important to God even if they felt like lost and wondering souls.

The second experience was in the prison hospital where a young man around 20-years-old was lying in bed recovering from a gunshot wound to the stomach. He was part of a shoot-out, he told me, and he walked away; not so his friend. After this prison visit, he and I began writing letters to each other—I wanted him to find purpose and direction for his life. I wanted him to find Jesus.

These stories were considered 'successes' when I shared them afterwards with the team. I never heard anything more about any of the fellows who had gathered in the bunk area to hear the story of the lost sheep. The exchange of letters between me and the injured inmate continued for about five or six months. When he left the prison hospital, I did not hear from him again.

While these were 'successes' in the minds of my co-laborers, I failed. I failed because I was so eager to tell what I knew, to share what I had found, but I never once—never!—bothered to talk to God about these men who were lost and hurt. Why would I not go to the Good Shepherd and ask the Shepherd to rescue these lost sheep? Was I so arrogant as to think I could rescue these lost sheep? Why not go to the "Great Physician" to ask for healing for the young man? Could I have possibly 'saved' him with my cunning and cleverly convincing arguments? As much as I talked to those men about God, I should have been talking to God about them. They never became a part of my prayer time.

Job's friends come and talk to him about God, about what he—Job—needs to do. They offer their insight, wisdom, and opinions. They talk for chapters to Job. But, do they ever stop and talk to God about Job? Do they lift to God their friend whom they have traveled so far to see and be with?

From my own experience since those early days in ministry, I find that true friends pray for one another. People who really care bring others before God in prayer. We bring the hurts and pains of those we love and want to help before God.

Scripture is full of this admonition and example:

> For this reason I kneel before the Father, from whom every family in heaven and on earth derives its name. I pray that out of his glorious riches he may strengthen you with power through his Spirit in your inner being, so that Christ may dwell in your hearts through faith. And I pray that you, being rooted and established in love, may have power, together with all the Lord's holy people, to grasp how wide and long and high and deep is the love of Christ, and to know this love that surpasses knowledge—that you may be filled to the measure of all the fullness of God. (Eph.3:14-19)

> For this reason, since the day we heard about you, we have not stopped praying for you. We continually ask God to fill you with the knowledge of his will through all the wisdom and understanding that the Spirit gives, so that you may live a life worthy of the Lord and please him in every way: bearing fruit in every good work, growing in the knowledge of God, being strengthened with all power according to his glorious might so that you may have great endurance and patience, and giving joyful thanks to the Father, who has qualified you to share in the inheritance of his holy people in the kingdom of light. (Col. 1:9-12)

> Therefore confess your sins to each other and pray for each other so that you may be healed. The prayer of a righteous person is powerful and effective.
> (James 5:16)

In John 17, Jesus prays for the disciples and for all believers (present and future). Jesus, Paul, and James show us that we pray for those who are dear to us, for those who are struggling, even for those who are opposed to us and opposed to the faith (Matt. 5:43-45).

Denise, one of the faithful members of a church I was serving some years ago, found herself quite suddenly in the hospital facing surgery. One of the first things she and her husband did was to contact me and ask me to pray. The morning of the surgery, she asked that we put a post on the church social media page asking people to pray. Denise and her husband understood the importance of our talking to God about those who suffer, those we care about.

In our moments of pain and need and hurt, we want people to pray for us. It may or may not be the time to talk to the person-in-need about God—sometimes being present is all that is needed—but it is always the right time to talk to God about the person-in-need.

Job's friends seem to have a lot to say to Job in this time of pain, but I wonder if they took the situation to God, if they spoke to God on Job's behalf? In the end, we find that Job does exactly this—he speaks to God on behalf of his friends. This is not a spoiler by jumping to the end of the book, but it does show us two important truths:

> [7]After the LORD had said these things to Job, he said to Eliphaz the Temanite, "I am angry with you and your two friends, because you have not spoken the truth about me, as my servant Job has. [8]So now take seven bulls and seven rams and go to my servant Job and sacrifice a burnt offering for yourselves. My servant Job will pray for you, and I will accept his prayer and not deal with you according to your folly. You have not spoken the truth about me, as my servant Job has." [9]So Eliphaz the Temanite, Bildad the Shuhite and Zophar

the Naamathite did what the LORD told them; and the
LORD accepted Job's prayer.   (Job 42:7-9)

The two important truths we see here are these:

1. The friends were quite definitely wrong about their understanding of God and the world—the 'retribution principle' is a false worldview. God tells the well-meaning friends, "You have not spoken the truth" about me. They did not 'lie;' they simply did not know the truth.

2. These three friends are helped, spared, because Job prays for them. Job prays for his friends.

On the Journey through Suffering—

We have already learned some important truths that can forever reshape the way we see our own lives and the world around us, and especially how we see suffering.

First of all, suffering, pain, hurt, and death are not tests or trials that God gives us, nor are they the result of "God's will." Let us quit blaming God for the bad stuff in our lives. Let us quit putting everything in this world on God. Besides giving God a bad rap, to do so is to deny the reality of evil—a reality our Bible clearly affirms.

Second, let us recognize that in this world powers and forces and beings act contrary to God and desire to undo any goodness that God pours out on the creation. These very real spiritual forces are arrayed against us in the Adversary, Satan—blame him! There is also the gift of free-will (truly a gift that allows us to choose, to love)— blame people's foolish or ignorant choices. One consequence of humanity's free-will is the general brokenness of our world.

Also, we recognize that friends can be an amazing source of comfort—do not pass up the chance to be a friend to someone in their moment of pain and suffering. Having someone nearby can make all the difference. Having a compassionate heart, a listening ear, or just being present in someone's suffering can mean so much.

One Friday afternoon, I called Marjan to see how she was doing. She was about half-way through her chemotherapy, and it has been doing a number on her. When she had her chemo, she usually was not back on her feet, so to speak, until some three days later. When I called on that Friday, she had had her chemo the previous day (I did not know they had changed it from Tuesday to Thursday). Even so, I could tell that she sounded ... strong. There was a lightness in her voice. Suddenly, as we talked, I heard a voice in the background. She told me that she was spending time at a friend's house, and from what I could hear, it was making all the difference in the world. Just being with people who cared about her seemed to be restorative. And, I was so happy for her!

When we are with people in their times of suffering, we may not know what to say to them. No problem. When our friends and loved ones are in pain, we may not need so much to talk to them; maybe that is when we need to talk to God about them.

Job is teaching us so much. No wonder the book of Job has endured the tests of time. What will Job teach us next?

Questions for Reflection—

1. Has there been a time you were tempted to "curse God"? What were you going through?

_____
_____
_____

2. Can you recall when having a friend or friends made all the difference in a difficult time?

_____
_____
_____

3. Have you been more ready to talk to others about God than to talk to God about others?

_____
_____
_____

Chapter 5
GETTING IT ALL OUT
JOB 3:1-26

The opening chapters of the book of Job have given us or reminded us of several truths that can help us better face—if not better endure—the suffering, the pain, the hurt of this world: God is not the Author of suffering; God allows the suffering in part because God has faith in us; and, the causes of suffering in this world are the forces of evil, our human free-will, and/or the consequences thereof.

This world and our lives in it—all created by our sovereign, omnipotent, all-powerful and good God—come with these sources of suffering mentioned above: Evil (the Satan, the Adversary, the Accuser, the Devil, forces of darkness, anything and everything contrary to God's good will) and human free-will—our ability to choose coupled with our own selfishness, arrogance, ill will, or ignorance (this on an individual level or corporate level or societal level). This free-will that allows us to love God and to love others, that allows us to choose what is good and right and helpful, has also led to our 'broken world,' a world beset by suffering. We find the story of our brokenness, of 'the Fall,' in Genesis 3. In the Genesis narrative, we learn that our broken world is the result of human free-will encouraged by evil—in the form of a serpent. These are the causes of suffering in our world.

Understanding these truths helps us in that we know that our suffering is not some arbitrary move by a capricious God out to torment us, and we know that there is someone or some force in this realm that wants us to suffer or at least to turn away from God (and our suffering may even be of our own doing). Knowing where the suffering comes from helps us to walk more confidently, faithfully, trustingly as God's people.

Let us see where this journey takes us as we look at the third chapter of Job.

Job is Having a Bad Day...

¹After this, Job opened his mouth and cursed the day of his birth. ²He said:

³"May the day of my birth perish, and the night that said, 'A boy is conceived!'

⁴That day—may it turn to darkness; may God above not care about it; may no light shine on it.

⁵May gloom and utter darkness claim it once more; may a cloud settle over it; may blackness overwhelm it.

⁶That night—may thick darkness seize it; may it not be included among the days of the year nor be entered in any of the months.

⁷May that night be barren; may no shout of joy be heard in it.

⁸May those who curse days curse that day, those who are ready to rouse Leviathan.

⁹May its morning stars become dark; may it wait for daylight in vain and not see the first rays of dawn, ¹⁰for

it did not shut the doors of the womb on me to hide
trouble from my eyes.   (Job 3:1-10)

First of all, we hear some very different words from what Job was saying earlier. When the raiders, soldiers, fires, and winds robbed him of his vast flocks and herds (his wealth) and children, how did our faithful man respond?

> The LORD gave and the LORD has taken away; may the name of the LORD be praised.   (Job 1:21b)

What has happened to Job's calm and confident response? What has happened to his 'accepting' answer to the horrors life (or in his mind, God) has handed him? Job seems to have changed his tune now. Why is that?

Well, as we see in Job 2, even more has happened to the man. Satan has stricken Job with "painful sores" from head to foot. He is now not only financially and emotionally carved out; he is in pain and surely wonders if this is the end.

His health is now threatened. His wife is fed up with it all. Though his well-meaning friends have arrived to be with him, everything is a mess.

Job's Lament

I am somewhat amused when some of the editors of the English Bible translations I have call this a "speech" in the editorial heading (remember, the original documents did not have editorial headings at the beginning of paragraphs or sections). Job's pouring forth is much more profound and painful than a mere 'speech.' This is lament—a passionate expression of grief, sorrow, and loss.[17]

---

[17] Oxford University Press (OUP). "Lament." *Lexico.Com*, 2021, www.lexico.com/en/definition/lament.

Job is crushed, empty, hurt—he is suffering. And he lets us know it. He allows his feelings to rise to the top. He is honest, painfully honest. His pain is so great, his loss so incredible, he wishes he were never born. I think he makes that very clear!

How do we react in our times of suffering? Are we willing to be as candid as Job?

Too many times, I have seen Christians who carry around a false piety from a misguided teaching that indicates something like, "I have Christ in my life; I have to be 'up' all the time!"

One of my colleagues in international mission ministry subscribed to this fallacy. After Mike had a mild heart-attack, he was back to work with the smile plastered to his face, telling everyone how good God is. In private, he and his wife were scared to death because they were far from what they considered adequate health care (living outside the US). Mike and his wife did not have the authenticity to reveal their very real fear in the situation, a situation—I might add—that warranted some fear and concern. Erroneously, they thought that admitting to suffering was somehow a sign of weakness. Job teaches us differently.

Have you known those folks who will not allow themselves to express their true negative feelings? Nothing is ever bad or wrong. Never will they let their guard down. They put on a smile, and not even the horrors of Job's life will wipe it off their faces. Too often, they bring that same face before God, or at least they are reluctant to pour out their pains and hurts to God. They and we often find it easier either to follow a rote recitation regarding "God's goodness" or focus on the positive instead of being real.

Job teaches us a different way. He shows us that it is okay to hurt, to mourn, and to suffer out loud. This last bit is very important. Job is not sitting alone here, musing over the suffering of his life. Job is not in prayer sharing this only with God. When we read this in context, we find that Job's friends are sitting with him—and have been for seven days. This verbal, audible outpouring indicates that we, too, need to voice our pains, our hurts, our losses not only to God but also to those close to us who are willing to hear our pain. We—like Job—need someone besides ourselves to know what we are feeling. This also means that if we happen to be one of the friends sitting close by, we need to let the one suffering cry out in pain or frustration.

How do we react to suffering—our own or someone else's?

Are we honest—like Job—or do we instead say what we think we should say? Do we really think that God (the omniscient One) would think less of us for expressing our pain or sorrow?

Do we allow others to express their pain, their hurt? Or, do we respond immediately with, "Oh, it'll get better!" "Look at the bright side!" "Think positive!" "Oh, don't say things like that!"

While these might be appropriate things to say at some point, I'm convinced—from what I read in Scripture, from what I have studied in psychology, and from my own years of experience in ministry—that people need to be able to have that moment when they can uninterruptedly moan, wail, weep, cry out, time to freely articulate the very real presence of the pain and suffering in their lives.

Where do ideas that 'we should keep it all in' or 'be positive all the time' come from? Where have we learned that we should not speak the truth about our feelings, our pain? Where have we learned to shut people down if they reveal the pain or darkness in their lives? Certainly, this does not come from Scripture! Moses, David, the Prophets, and Jesus all let God have it and let the world know it—they poured out their hearts, their pains, and their disappointment.

David is one who teaches us over and over throughout the Psalms that crying out honestly to God should be a part of our prayer life:

> [1]My God, my God, why have you forsaken me?
> Why are you so far from saving me,
> so far from my cries of anguish?
> [2]My God, I cry out by day, but you do not answer,
> by night, but I find no rest.   (Ps. 22:1-2)

Paul writes openly about a "thorn in the flesh"—a source of suffering that he begs God to remove (II Cor.12:7-10). Rather than hide his pain, he admits it. Jesus—the Son of God, Saviour of the World—cries out in fear (Matt. 26:39) and in pain (Matt. 27:45-50). None of the disciples approached him in the garden saying, "Oh, Jesus, look on the bright side...!" No. People throughout Scripture voice their anguish, their pain, and they allow others to do the same. Are they not models for us today?

Now, something important to note is that none of these people "parks" there. They experience pain and suffering, they articulate it, but they do not remain there. We do not want to become that other extreme—the perpetual purveyors of bad news with a constant litany of "woe is me." We do not want to be or be around those who continually lament, day after day after day. But, we need to be able to experience and voice the sufferings if and when they come to our lives. And, we need to give others the space to do the same. With the examples above from Scripture, why would we think we should do anything less?

Job's honest lament, his candid response to all of the horrors of his life, provides an excellent example for us and frees us to bring our deepest hurts, fears, and anger to God, knowing that God will hear us and love us—regardless. Job's example also shows us again the importance of having friends and being friends for others, of having friends around us and being friends for others who will hear the cry of pain. We are free to cry, to hurt, to mourn before God and friends, and God will think none the less of us. And, we should think none the less of each other.

God's Doing?

While Job freely opens up and raises his lament to God, he still thinks that all of this is somehow the work of God. We see this in the midst of his lament:

> [20]"Why is light given to those in misery,
>   and life to the bitter of soul,
> [21]to those who long for death that does not come,
>   who search for it more than for hidden treasure,
> [22]who are filled with gladness
>   and rejoice when they reach the grave?
> [23]Why is life given to a man
>   whose way is hidden,
>   whom God has hedged in?   (Job 3:20-23)

At the end of the final verse quoted here, Job's attitude—his understanding and worldview—slips in: "…whom God has hedged in." God had done this. God has robbed him of his children, his flocks (wealth), and his health.

Who perhaps would not have felt this way living in a culture steeped in the worldview of the 'retribution principle'? Who would not feel this way even today if they had not yet been shown the grace and mercy of a loving God as revealed in Scripture, in Jesus? Perhaps this worldview is simply 'natural' to us—a belief that whatever happens is as a result of God's doing.

We must keep in mind that Job is on a spiritual journey in this ancient story. He is in a process of growth and change. While he and his friends occupy a similar space theologically and philosophically in these opening chapters of the book, Job ends up in a different place from his friends. Job is learning—slowly but surely. Job's eyes are opening—little by little. Even as we crave grace from others, let us show Job grace as this narrative gets under way.

Jesus on Suffering

Unfortunately, though Job ends at a different place at the end of the book in his name, the followers of his friends—Eliphaz, Bildad, and Zophar—persist. They walked with Jesus and even remain with us today.

In that insightful passage in the New Testament where Jesus and the disciples encounter a blind man, or more specifically, a man born blind, the disciples ask Jesus who sinned to cause his blindness.

> [1]As [Jesus] went along, he saw a man blind from birth. [2]His disciples asked him, "Rabbi, who sinned, this man or his parents, that he was born blind?" (John 9:1-2)

Yes, the disciples of Eliphaz, Bildad, and Zophar remain in the world—people who think that if someone is sick or hurt or suffering, it is because they have sinned or someone close to them has sinned. If someone is experiencing something bad, it must be due to their own doing with relation to God. We see this clearly in the disciples' question: "Whose sin caused this man's blindness?" Who did what to result in this living tragedy? They still hold on to the idea of 'the good are blessed; the bad are cursed."

We are tempted to do the same. Often, when we see someone suffer in some way, we wonder why God is punishing them. Unfortunately, this attitude and worldview remain alive and well even in the Church today. So many Christians want to assign a simple 'cause and effect' explanation to our suffering.

In my own adult life, I have heard and seen people with a national microphone imply or say that an individual's suffering is generally a direct result of their personal sin. Scripture is very clear: Job's suffering is not a result of his sin. Many people suffer because of sin generally, but not from their own sins. While many suffer because of sin (actions and attitudes contrary to the wishes and will of God), we simply cannot positively correlate my suffering with my sin or your suffering with your sin.

When the tsunami hit Thailand in 2005, some Christian leaders spoke of God's punishment on a non-Christian nation. When the earthquake destroyed much of Haiti in 2010, some Christian leaders stood to declare that this is what happens to a nation when its people practice witchcraft. Even as I write these words, COVID-19 devastates the United States, and televangelists and leading Christian pastors attribute this to God.

John Piper, one of the leading voices of conservative Christianity in America, someone whose books I have read and appreciated, had this to say about the COVID pandemic: "God sometimes uses disease to bring particular judgments upon those who reject him and give themselves over to sin...."[18] Wow. Piper—at least at the moment he was asked about the pandemic—remained where Job was at the beginning of his journey, and Piper is a 21st Century leader of faith in America. No wonder so many 21st Century AD Christians are still holding on to a 20th Century BC worldview!

In my reading of Scripture, when God sees tsunamis, earthquakes, pandemics, when God sees cancer, murders, and beatings, God weeps. If Jesus wept over the loss of one person and the pain the family suffered (John 11:32ff), I am fairly certain that God's heart breaks with ours over the suffering of the world.

---

[18] Jonathon Merritt. "Some of the Most Visible Christians in America are Failing the Coronavirus Test." *The Atlantic*, April 24, 2020.
https://www.theatlantic.com/ideas/archive/2020/04/christian-cruelty-face-covid-19/610477/.

So, Jesus' disciples also reveal through their question their own belief that this man's blindness is something caused by God as punishment for some sin.

Jesus, however, is very clear in his answer:

> ³"Neither this man nor his parents sinned," said Jesus, "but this happened so that the works of God might be displayed in him. ⁴As long as it is day, we must do the works of him who sent me. Night is coming, when no one can work. ⁵While I am in the world, I am the light of the world." (John 9:3-5)

No one's sin caused this blindness. He is blind because he is blind, born into a broken world—no blame to go around. But, as Jesus also indicates and our experiences bear out, God can and will work in the midst of or through the sickness, pain, and suffering of our lives. We have that amazing, infinitely comforting promise that Paul writes in Roman 8:28—"And we know that all things work together for good to those who love God, to those who are the called according to His purpose" (NKJV).

God will take the broken, hurtful, painful things in our lives and turn them around "for the good." In fact, when those difficult times do come, God usually gets a bit more of our attention than on those sunny, care-free days of life. Who of us has not found ourselves sick—the flu or worse—and suddenly our prayer-life moves up to the next level?

When our family served in Venezuela, I contracted dengue fever—also called 'bone-break fever.' I had never had anything like that in my life. My friend, Samuel, and I had gone 'in country' to visit a mission that was springing up in the city of Barinas. On the first day, we were out and about all day, and that evening we attended an open-air worship at the home of one of the local mission leaders.

When we got up to leave at the end of our time there, I awoke feeling a little 'under the weather.' As we drove the six hour trip home to Barquisimeto, the fever increased. Within a day or two, the pain set in. This was no ordinary pain! The pain was unimaginably excruciating—I did not curse the day of my birth as Job did, but I did truly and earnestly pray for the Lord to take me, to just let me die! I can promise you, my prayer life went from a four to a ten in no time flat.

God did not cause my illness, God does not cause other illnesses, God does not cast pain and hurt and loss into our lives, God does not rob us of health and happiness—God, as Scripture tells us time and again, is the Author of life and hope and goodness! But, there is an Adversary, the Satan, who is crouching in wait to devour us (I Peter 5:8). We do live in a broken world that includes illness, sickness, injury, and heartbreak. We are a people prone to selfishness, arrogance, egotism, and greed—and these impact our lives and the lives of others. But, we have a God who promises to take all of the resulting hurt, pain, and suffering and work through them for 'good.'

As indicated before, our own free-will choices bring us at times to self-destructive, harmful decisions. When I was seven years old, my friends and I thought it would be fun and clever to be the 'kissing tire bike team'—riding up close and sliding the front tire of one bike up against the side of the back tire of another bike ... as we were riding down the road. This was our choice, our decision, and the two-inch scar on my right knee is still visible today. God did not do that. Forces of evil did not do that. The forces of gravity and a bad decision did that.

While my bike incident did not bring me closer to God, I did learn something about being cautious. My 'critical thinking' skills definitely leveled up. We learn from our suffering.

When I was studying at the Candler School of Theology at Emory University, I took a class on 'morality'—a heady course looking at the sources of our moral inclinations and moral behavior. While I don't recall many of the details from the course, a conversation from that class has stuck with me forever.

One of my classmates was a kindly, elderly Greek Orthodox priest, Father Mike. He was funny and gentle and honest. One morning, I came to class and Fr. Mike could see that I was preoccupied.

"Jon, what's up?" he asked.

"We got word last night that my mother-in-law had a stroke ... and it doesn't look good," I responded.

"Oh, I'm so sorry..."

"Yeah. We only hope that she doesn't have to suffer."

"Is she a person of faith?"

"Not really..."

"Well, maybe she needs to suffer."

Who says that? But, he was exactly right. Now that we know that suffering can push us towards God, maybe there are times and moments when people need to suffer. Maybe there have been times when you and I needed to experience a bit of suffering to nudge us back towards God. Again, I do not believe God causes suffering, but God uses the suffering for our good.

Suffering is not the work of God. Our suffering may have been influenced by the evil forces in the world (we would like to say, "The Devil made me do it!"), but by and large, suffering is often the result of our free-will, our bad choices. Regardless of the source of the suffering, God is there to care for us, to hear us, to bring healing, to bring hope, to give us strength. Yes, God can even work good through the foolishness of our lives. And God can definitely draw us closer through the suffering of our lives.

In the New Testament passage from Luke 9 that we looked at above, God uses a young man's blindness to reveal the truth of God in Christ Jesus, to open spiritual eyes of the people around this man. Two thousand years later, this passage continues to open our spiritual eyes to God's goodness

On the Journey through Suffering—

Job—the book and the man—is teaching us a lot!

Since repetition is the mother of learning, we do well to remember all that the book of Job is teaching us.

First, we see clearly that suffering, pain, hurt, and death are not "gifts" that God gives us nor are they punishments that God slams on us—let us quit blaming God for the bad stuff in our lives.

Then, we also see in the book of Job—confirmed in various passages and by various writers in the Old and New Testaments—that there are very real spiritual forces arrayed against us ... like the Adversary, Satan. If we want to blame someone for the pains of this life, blame Satan! There's also free-will or choice that God blesses Adam and Eve (and all humanity) with when they are created and placed in Garden ('free-will' is a blessing—it allows us to choose God, to follow Jesus, but it also allows us to reject God and ignore Jesus). So, besides evil forces, we can also blame our own foolish or ignorant choices for our suffering, or the choices of those who have gone before us or who act around us for whose sinful (evil, selfish, or ignorant) decisions we suffer today.

We also find in our study of Job that friends can be an amazing source of comfort—we should not pass up the chance to be with someone in their moment of pain and suffering. It is not about words; it is about being present and recognizing the pain of friends in their suffering.

We are reminded that a time of suffering is not necessarily improved by our improvised, well-meaning 'sermons.' When our friends and loved ones are in pain, let us not just talk to them about God; let us talk to God about them. In the midst of their suffering is always the right time to pray for those who suffer.

And in this chapter, we learn that those who are suffering, those in pain, can cry out, scream, yell, lament—pain and suffering are part and parcel of this world, and we do well to express it. We should feel free to cry out to God in the presence of trusted friends. And, if we are the trusted friends, we need to allow those who suffer to cry out, to share with us the pain of their lives. What we find is that God often speaks to our hearts most clearly when we are in those times of pain, suffering, and hurt.

My friend, Marjan, finds herself far from home. Her mother is of fragile health, so she has not even told her parents of what she is going through. Her older sister is 1200 miles away in Canada. She has few friends. Our phone calls have been a chance for her to unload, to express her pain, to express her frustrations. Those moments are few, but she feels free to rant—and I am happy to let her do that.

The Sunday I preached the sermon that serves as a foundation of this chapter, we came to the Table to remember Jesus, one who had suffered beyond anything we can imagine. He suffered not because he was sinful or wrong or bad. He suffered not because his Father was capricious or inflicting some disciplinary or didactic torture on him. He suffered because Roman soldiers nailed him to a cross. He suffered because some of the Jewish leaders were frightened of this simple Galilean who was moving the masses with his message of God's Kingdom. He suffered for us and because of us and our sin, and he suffered that we might know God and have a different kind of life because of his life and death.

This is a mystery: Somehow, the work of Jesus on the Cross makes a way for us to know God and become a part of God's family and God's mission to the world, a mission of hope, peace, grace, and love. That is the kind of God in whom we trust, in whom we hope, and in whom we learn to love.

Questions for Reflection—

1. Have you grown up in a culture that urges you to "suffer in silence"?

___

2. Have you been prone to look for sin in the lives of those you see suffering?

___

3. When have you seen God bring something good out of suffering?

___

Chapter 6
"WITH FRIENDS LIKE THESE…?"
JOB 4 – 13

The original sermon series that serves as a basis for this book does not include these chapters or any readings from these chapters, so feel free to jump to the next chapter. I have decided not to ignore these chapters because they drive home to misunderstanding of Job's friends, a misunderstanding that still pervades our world. Important insight comes out of these chapters that clarify where Job's friends stand and where Job stands. First, let us take a look at the friends and the 'wisdom' they bring to their suffering friend.

Is there Any Wisdom?

After cajoling Job for whining a bit in his situation, Eliphaz lays out his own worldview for all to see:

> 7"Consider now: Who, being innocent, has ever perished?
> Where were the upright ever destroyed?
> (Job 4:7)

In what world does Eliphaz live? In my own lifetime, I have seen over and over and over the upright destroyed and the innocent perishing. Any 'natural disaster' or human disaster we mention will have upright and innocent suffering. In every war, the innocent suffer.

During the days I was writing this chapter, a huge explosion rocked the city of Beirut in Lebanon (August 2020). In the first days after the explosion, no one was sure why or how this port building exploded. What we did know was that over 150 died and thousands had been directly impacted.

Particularly heart-wrenching for me was seeing video footage of a wedding photo-shoot that was happening nearby when the explosion happened. [19] The joy of the young bride is unquestionably clear on her face, matching—I am sure—the happiness on the faces of family members. And then, a shudder of the camera ... and the shock wave from the explosion passes through the open courtyard. A moment later after the camera is righted, we see the destruction, the cries, the shock, the mess of tangled tables and decorations—heartbreaking. The innocent suffer.

If that is not enough, how do we apply Eliphaz' declaration to the nine-month-old baby who dies of COVID-19 in the hospital near where I live in the Rio Grande Valley? How do we tell that family 'the good live and the bad die'? Is there any way that this precious nine-month-old baby girl was 'evil' or could have 'sowed trouble'? The innocent suffer.

So, Eliphaz, I tell you this young bride preparing joyfully for marriage is just one of thousands of examples of the innocent suffering in this one disaster in a city of Lebanon. Eliphaz, this small child dying of COVID in the hospital near my home is exactly the innocent you talk about, one of the millions who suffers unjustly.

---

[19] Reuters. "Beirut Explosion Rocks Bride's Photoshoot." *YouTube*, uploaded by Reuters, 5 Aug. 2020, www.youtube.com/watch?v=_L7SlqDtRnc.

And, are you also going to say, Eliphaz, that God has done these things?

We see people all the time in the news who live horrific lives yet enjoy wealth and fame. Just look as the world of Hollywood where drugs, gratuitous sex, and egocentrism seem to reign as the actors reap wealth and power. Where is their harvest of suffering? And, we also see around us those who live well, who keep the rules, and yet they suffer.

In August of 2019, we witnessed two widely publicized mass shootings in the United States—one in El Paso, Texas, and one in Dayton, Ohio. In El Paso, a shooter motivated by racism and political rhetoric randomly shot and killed 23 people and injured 23 others. In Dayton, the shooter killed nine people and wounded 17 others. What terrific evil did those people do who fell to the bullets of the racist shooter? And those who fell to the Dayton shooter—what did they do that merited sudden death? Were they all reaping the harvest of their lives? I cannot imagine any person in their right mind suggesting such a thing. Yet, Eliphaz suggests exactly this with regard to Job's suffering—"You've got what was coming to you!"

In Job 5, Eliphaz continues:

> [17]"Blessed is the one whom God corrects;
> so do not despise the discipline of the Almighty.
> [18]For he wounds, but he also binds up;
> he injures, but his hands also heal.
>
> (Job 5:17-18)

Before we latch onto this as "truth," we must remember—or if not remember, at least be aware—that at the end of Job, Eliphaz is going to be reprimanded for his false counsel, for being a bad friend, for telling Job what is not true. He shares his thoughts and ideas with good intention, completely convinced of his own worldview, sure of his 'rightness.' Yet, he is wrong. And Job seems to have a sense now that his friend is wrong.

Job Responds to Eliphaz

In Job 6 and 7, Job responds to Eliphaz—sort of. In fact, he seems to be talking as if his friends are not even there. In a way, the friends were a greater comfort when they just sat there with their mouths closed. (We need to remember this.)

First of all, in Job 6, Job the man simply wants his life to end. His suffering seems to be too much. Some of us have been to that place, that place of pain and hurt and suffering that leads us to wonder if it might not be a little easier to simply step out of this world and enjoy the heavenly rest of the after-life. Since we are dealing with suffering, we must deal with this issue.

Job responds to his suffering in the following manner. And, if Job is someone to emulate, then we, too, can get to the end our rope and cry out to God in the same way:

> 8"Oh, that I might have my request,
>   that God would grant what I hope for,
> 9that God would be willing to crush me,
>   to let loose his hand and cut off my life!
> (Job 6:8-9)

Job is ready to die. Enough of this suffering! "Cut off my life!" Yet in the midst of his suffering, he is not ready to end his own life. He is not at a point where he thinks he can take his own life. But, he is willing to let God take his life—this distinction is important.

Today, our society and culture are wrestling with the questions of 'euthanasia': Is it ever right or okay to take one's own life to avoid or end suffering? Often this is called 'mercy killing.' We have seen stories of those who were sick, dying, or thinking they were dying, who opted for 'assisted suicide.'

In the 1990's our newspapers and news magazines (prior to 24/7 cable news sources!) were filled with stories and opinion pieces about Dr. Jack Kevorkian. He was 'helping' people end their lives of suffering. He even developed a 'suicide machine.'[20] Yet, Job never thinks of taking his own life. May Job serve as an example for us. He is simply ready for God to allow him to die or for God to simply take his life.

Not only is Job ready to die; he is ready for his friends to die, or at least take a hike. They have hammered Job unceasingly with this 'retribution' theology, certain that Job's state of affairs is simply his just dues for something he has done.

In his frustration, Job addresses his "friends":

> [14]"Anyone who withholds kindness from a friend
> forsakes the fear of the Almighty.
> [15]But my brothers are as undependable as
> intermittent streams,
> as the streams that overflow…
> [20]They are distressed, because they had been
> confident…
> [21]Now you too have proved to be of no help….
> (Job 6:14-21)

Job calls these fellows "undependable" and "no help." Take off, fellows, with your words of judgment and calls for repentance. Job is more certain of himself; he knows himself, and he knows that his friends are offering nothing useful, nothing helpful in the midst of his suffering.

But the message of his friends—the 'retribution principle'—has had an effect on Job. He wonders if he has done something. Maybe they are right? So, he questions God:

> [20]If I have sinned, what have I done to you,
> you who see everything we do?

---

[20] "Suicide Machines." *Dr. Jack Kevorkian: Euthanasia and Physician Assisted Suicide*, 2012, euthanasian.weebly.com/suicide-machines.html.

> Why have you made me your target?
>> Have I become a burden to you?
> ²¹Why do you not pardon my offenses
>> and forgive my sins?
> For I will soon lie down in the dust;
>> you will search for me, but I will be no more."
>>> (Job 7:20-21)

Perhaps Job thinks that he should take out a bit of "fire insurance"—just in case. Yet, he does not show signs of 'turning,' of admitting to any wrong-doing. If anything, he is sticking firmly to his story and asking God to show him what he cannot see in his own life: "I'm almost dead—I don't get it. Show me what I've done wrong." He is willing to see his mistakes, willing to own them if they are there, but he really does not know of any sin in his life. So why is he suffering? He and we will get to the bottom of this.

Bildad Speaks

Meanwhile, Bildad takes over the narrative, but continues with the same message: You have messed up, Job, and you just need to repent.

> ²"How long will you say such things?
>> Your words are a blustering wind.
> ³Does God pervert justice?
>> Does the Almighty pervert what is right?
> ⁴When your children sinned against him,
>> he gave them over to the penalty of their sin.
> ⁵But if you will seek God earnestly
>> and plead with the Almighty,
> ⁶if you are pure and upright,
>> even now he will rouse himself on your behalf
>> and restore you to your prosperous state.

> ⁷Your beginnings will seem humble,
> so prosperous will your future be.
>
> (Job 8:2-7)

There it is again, that 'retribution principle'—"Your kids got what was coming to them!" (v.4) and "if you are pure and upright" (v.6), God will come to your aid.

God punishes the bad and rewards the good in these people's worldview. And while we love this message on our good days and in our good moments, while we love this message when we see the vile and evil in the news, we really do not want this to be the case when we slip up, when we fall into the pit of sin. When we are the rebellious ones, when we are wrong, when we are selfish, and we are sinful, we strain our ears to hear about mercy, grace, and forgiveness. Hear what Jesus says:

> "This is what God does. He gives his best—the sun to warm and the rain to nourish—to everyone, regardless: the good and bad, the nice and nasty."
>
> (Matthew 5:45, The Message)[21]

Jesus' message is clear. Jesus' understanding of how God acts is clear—God is good. God blesses. God sends the good in our lives.

Oh, if we could but maintain a consistent standard! If only we would measure the world by the standard we wish to be measured by. Didn't Jesus have something to say about that as well, something about dealing with others the way we want to be dealt with, something about 'doing unto others as we would have them do unto us'…? (Matt. 7:12).

---

[21] Eugene Peterson. *The Message New Testament with Psalms and Proverbs*. 1st ed., (NavPress Publishing Group, 2007).

In Job 9 and 10, Job begins to question where all of this suffering is coming from. In frustration, he cries out, "If it is not [God], then who is it?" (9:24b).

Of course, we must now be aware that we—you and I—have been given privy information. We were able to see 'behind the curtain,' if you will, in Job 1 & 2, and there we learn that there are other forces at play in this narrative. We see and hear the Accuser—Satan—taunting God and condemning Job. We know the answer to "who is it?" We know there are evil forces in the world that are not concerned about blessing the good and only cursing the bad. We know there are powers that want anything and everything that is contrary to God's will and wishes. Job does not know this. Job has not seen this. So, he is understandably confused.

Job has lived with and in this world of the 'retribution principle' all of his life. Never has he faced as much loss, destruction, and suffering as he has now. Yet, he knows that what his friends are preaching to him does not sit well. He is sure of his innocence. Job cries out to God, "...You know that I am not guilty" (Job 10:4). Job is certain of his innocence and confused by his experience. Well, at least we all have this last piece in common. How many times have we cried out, "Why me?" Our experiences leave us questioning.

Recently, I saw a post from a dear friend on social media who related that their car was re-ended. My friend was mildly injured and would not be able to engage in their favorite exercise program for some weeks. At the end of the post, my friend declared, "God's timing is always perfect!"

So, let me get this right: God planned this rear-ending at just the right time? God robbed you of your favorite way to stay healthy at just the right moment? Really? Could it be possible that there is another force at work in your life taking away the joys, that maybe—just maybe—God is not the one stealing the goodness out of your life? Is it possible—just possible—that you were rear-ended because someone decided that texting a cute smiley-face to a friend was more important than paying attention to the road?

We are sitting with Job in the ashes hearing all of the well-meaning people saying things like, "Well, God's timing is perfect." "God knows what He's doing!" "God always takes the best ones first...." Too often we are surrounded by friends as well intentioned as Job's, and just as wrong as Job's.

Zophar Remains Wrong ... So Far!

Another friend, Zophar, speaks up in Job 11. He knows that Job must be either hiding something or simply forgetting something:

> ⁴You say to God, 'My beliefs are flawless
> and I am pure in your sight.'
> ⁵Oh, how I wish that God would speak,
> that he would open his lips against you....
> (Job 11:-4-5)

Zophar, like Job, wants God to speak (just hold on, folks—God will speak!), but Zophar wants God to speak against Job, not for Job. What kind of friend is that?

Job has had enough, and in Job 12, he finally lets loose on his friends who think they are so wise:

> ⁴You, however, smear me with lies;
> you are worthless physicians, all of you!
> ⁵If only you would be altogether silent!
> For you, that would be wisdom.
> (Job 12:4-5)

Just shut up already! Job has some choice words for these friends. Certainly, Job would agree with that old saying, "With friends like you, who needs enemies?"

All Job really wants is a moment with God, a moment to talk and explain and listen and learn. Hear Job's words from Chapter 13:

> ¹³"Keep silent and let me speak;
> then let come to me what may.
> ¹⁴Why do I put myself in jeopardy
> and take my life in my hands?
> ¹⁵Though [God] slay me, yet will I hope in him;
> I will surely defend my ways to his face.
> (Job 13:13-15)

On the Journey through Suffering

First, we do see Job's unwavering faith here—"Though [God] slay me, yet will I hope in him" (13:15a). Still, Job wants his chance to make his case before God as well. He is sure that he has not done anything to anger God. He is certain of his own innocence.

While not "innocent," my friend, Marjan, has expressed similar frustrations. During one of our phone conversations, she cried out, "It's not fair! I'm not perfect, but I don't deserve this!" I agreed with her. Who deserves cancer? Loss of love? Loneliness? Crushed dreams? Who of us has not cried out in the same way?

While we do not share the certainty of our innocence (in fact, as Christians, we are certain of the opposite—of our guilt, of our sinfulness, of our unworthiness), we still stand before the universe crying out for justice or at least an explanation. We know there is something 'not right,' and we know now with certainty that God is not causing all of the pain. While we do not share Job's sense of innocence, perhaps we can share his faith, his certainty, his confidence in God.

Looking around the world we live in, hearing the words of the New Testament, we realize what Job's friends refuse to admit—everyone suffers. The good, the bad, and everyone in between suffers. Our suffering—again—is not based on our goodness or badness. We suffer because we live in a broken world. Our loved ones suffer because we live in a broken world. But suffering is not the end of the story.

Some of the final words here carry us forward into the next chapter of our journey: "...Yet will I hope in him." Why, Job? If you think this suffering is of God, why would you hope in God? Is it because you know that all of the good things in your life came from God?

Hope—this is, in fact, one of the keys for our survival in midst of our lives of suffering.

Questions for Reflection—

1. Has anyone ever suggested that your suffering was God's judgement on you? Did you agree?

_____
_____
_____

2. Have you seen others suffering and wondered if it was God's doing? Could there have been other sources of their suffering?

_____
_____
_____

3. If suffering drives someone to suicide, could that suffering come from God?

_____
_____
_____

Chapter 7
HOPE = LIFE!
JOB 14:7-15

The book of Job is such an important part of Scripture because these 42 chapters of text take us on a journey through suffering. We all experience suffering, pain, loss, hurt, and we want answers. As I write these words, the world continues to grapple with the COVID-19 pandemic and the millions of lives lost. I imagine we will be dealing with the fallout from this pandemic for years to come. No country, it seems, is spared the violence of this virus. China, Italy, France, Spain, Brazil, India, and the U.S. seem to be especially hard hit at this time, and we do not know how this will end. The physical suffering parallels economic hardships affecting hundreds of thousands of businesses and millions of families.

Closer to home, the United States faces the systemic racism that has been exposed through the tragic and senseless deaths of George Floyd, Breonna Taylor, Abmaud Arbery, and too many others. Their deaths have resulted in protests and riots as generations of frustration and fear finally boil to the surface. America is today a different place as the suffering shifts the very ground under our perceived reality.

Countless of our friends and family members have battled or are battling cancer or other debilitating or life-threatening illnesses. Jobs are lost. Homes burn down. Storms wash neighborhoods away. And, the person we love gets up one day and unexpectedly walks out the door.

We all want explanations. We reason that if we can figure out what causes the pain in our lives, we might be able to avoid the suffering or at least lessen the suffering. If we can observe Job's life—one who goes through the fires of suffering (the worst kinds!) and comes out okay on the other side, if we can discover some nugget of wisdom for living from Job's life, maybe we can navigate the sufferings of our own lives better.

Yes, Job the man dealt with pain and suffering. As we go through the book of Job, as we walk along with Job (and his 'friends'), we gain a deeper and better understanding of both suffering and faithful living.

At the beginning of the narrative, Job loses his property, his herds, and his family—his children. In the face of all his loss, he mistakenly thinks that God is the author of his suffering and declares, "The LORD gave and the LORD has taken away; may the name of the LORD be praised" (Job 1:21b).

He has it half right. The LORD does give, does bless, and the LORD may take away at times, but what was taken from Job was taken by Satan.

We may or may not get things 'half right' as Job did, but we often get things upside-down. How many times have we moaned when things did not go our way, "Why is God doing this to me?!"

Our son, Andrew, was learning to ride his scooter when he was three years old. He had practiced a route that ran from the side driveway, around the big oak tree, and down the sidewalk in front of the house. He had done it time and again, so many times.

One day, we were outside with the video camera. "Dad, record this!" So, I did. As he rounded the tree, his little front wheel fell right into a crack and stopped dead. My son and the rest of scooter spilled over head-first smack on to the sidewalk. He came up wailing. As we consoled him, he cried, "God made me do it!" Grateful for the theological moment, I steered him in a better direction.

But, some folks never get beyond where my three-year-old son was that day—when bad things come along, they cry out in all seriousness, truly believing, "Why is God doing this to me?!"

Perhaps just as bad as or worse than blaming God for every hurt and pain is how we act or react when good things come our way. When the good things come along in life, we tend to take a deep breath, put on a little swagger, and declare, "Man, I am GOOD!" That special someone agrees to go out on a date, and we respond, "Yeah, I got it!" We work a good "deal" buying something we need—a car, a fridge, a suit, a dress, a blouse—and announce, "I can deal it, I can deal it!" For some strange, mixed up reason, we think we are good—or great! We think we make the good things happen in our lives.

We have things so upside-down: The bad is from God; the good is from our own amazing selves? In a right-side-up world, we would recognize what Scripture points out, that "every good and perfect gift comes down from the Father of heavenly lights" (James 1:17), and every pain, mess, disaster grows out of the work of Satan, the brokenness of this world, or our own (or others) foolish or thoughtless decisions.

The book of Job, like the Epistle of James, teaches us that God is the Author of all things good, and Job also shows us that there are forces in this world that wish us harm and that the brokenness of our world and our decisions lead us to disaster at times.

A Shift—from Lament to…?

Job continues a slow transformation:

> ⁷"At least there is hope for a tree: If it is cut down, it will sprout again, and its new shoots will not fail.
>
> ⁸Its roots may grow old in the ground and its stump die in the soil, 9yet at the scent of water it will bud and put forth shoots like a plant.
>
> ¹⁰ But a man dies and is laid low; he breathes his last and is no more.
>
> ¹¹As the water of a lake dries up or a riverbed becomes parched and dry, ¹²so he lies down and does not rise; till the heavens are no more, people will not awake or be roused from their sleep.
>
> ¹³"If only you would hide me in the grave and conceal me till your anger has passed! If only you would set me a time and then remember me!
>
> ¹⁴If someone dies, will they live again? All the days of my hard service I will wait for my renewal to come.
>
> ¹⁵You will call and I will answer you; you will long for the creature your hands have made." (Job 14:7-15)

In the opening verses of this passage (vs. 7-9), Job considers a tree. He points out that the tree seems to find new life even after it seems dead.

When we returned from being out of town at youth camp one July, I noticed that there had been small fire at the edge of a field near the Stripes gas-station/food-mart close to where we lived then in Rio Grande City, Texas. The ground was scorched, and a lone mesquite tree was burned black. I remember thinking, "Ah…bad time for that in the middle of the dry season—that'll be burnt and dead until the next rains in September." I was wrong.

Just two weeks later as I passed that patch of ground, I was surprised and pleased to see that new grass had sprouted, the mesquite tree was covered in green leaves, and some weeds were slowly covering over the scar of the fire. Evidently, the fire had burned off the surface of the ground, but the roots and seeds in the ground were still there. Job was right—these plants and trees can return with new life.

Then, Job shifts from the tree to consider humankind (vs.10-13). What about people? No new life there! Once we are knocked down, once we are stripped of life, there is no renewal. When we are done, we are done. When we are burned out and cut down, we humans do not tend to rise again. And, we can easily imagine that Job feels burned out, stripped bare, cut down—he senses that when he is dead, he will be dead.

We have, no doubt, felt the same way at times. Someone reading this may be feeling scorched and burned out even now. But, as Job goes on, he realizes and reminds us that this is not the end.

In verses 14-15, we sense a change, a shift. Job realizes that he is not dead yet. He may be sitting in ashes, but he is not completely burned out. His world has been cut down, but he is not cut down completely. He has voice, he has thought, and as long as he is alive, he has hope! The tree may live again, and humankind may find no new life, but Job declares a message for himself and for us: As long as I live, there is hope!

We hear this again clearly later in Job's discourse in Job 19:

> [23]"Oh, that my words were recorded, that they were written on a scroll,
> [24]that they were inscribed with an iron tool on lead or engraved in rock forever!
> [25]I know that my redeemer lives, and that in the end he will stand on the earth.
> [26]And after my skin has been destroyed, yet in my flesh I will see God;

²⁷I myself will see him with my own eyes—I, and not another. How my heart yearns within me! (Job 19:23-27)

In the midst of his sorrow, loss and suffering, Job holds on to hope. In fact, we should not even be surprised. He is a man of faith, after all, a man of unwavering faith, and a large measure of faith has to do with hope. Do you know or recall the words Paul wrote to the Christians who lived and suffered in Rome?

> ...We know that suffering produces perseverance; perseverance, character; and character, hope. And hope does not put us to shame, because God's love has been poured out into our hearts through the Holy Spirit, who has been given to us. (Romans 5:3-5)

Suffering produces perseverance which produces character which produces hope! Job knows what suffering is. His suffering resulted in perseverance, character ... and now hope! His journey through suffering, loss, and pain has brought him to a new place. Job has HOPE! And hope? Well, hope is everything.

The Power of Hope

Patrick Seger was the Samaritan's Purse team leader in the Philippines for the first month after Typhoon Haiyan hit the country in 2013. "The typhoon's fury affected more than 14 million people across 44 provinces, displacing 4.1 million people, killing more than 6,000 people, and leaving 1,800 missing. In addition, 1.1 million houses were either partially or totally damaged, 33 million coconut trees (a major source of livelihoods) were destroyed, and the livelihoods of 5.9 million workers were disrupted." [1]

---

[1] "From the Field: 2013 Typhoon Haiyan: Facts, FAQs, and how to help." World Vision. https://www.worldvision.org/disaster-relief-news-stories/2013-typhoon-haiyan-facts

In the face of this level of destruction and suffering, here are some of Seger's thoughts:

> "It's been said that a person can live 40 days without food, four days without water, four minutes without air, but only four seconds without hope. Why? Hope provides the power that energizes us with life. Hope is a powerful thing. It keeps us going when times are tough. It creates excitement in us for the future. It gives us reason to live. It gives us strength and courage." [2]

Seger's message: Hope gives us life in the face of suffering.

Also in 2013, Time magazine published an article entitled "How Hope Works." [3] The author, Jeffrey Kluger, points to scientific data, psychological experiments, and very real, everyday experiences of people in order to show first of all that there is a direct link between hope and work productivity and academic achievement. The author points out that hope is not the same as wishing. Hope is a deliberate process that recognizes where one is, where one wants to be, and a willingness to take the steps to get from one place to the other.[4] Studies found that people with a higher level of hope had a greater tolerance for discomfort, inconvenience, and suffering. Hope has power!

In 2015, The New York Times published "The Power of Hope is Real."[5] Kristof, the author, points to multinational studies that have shown that people who are stressed, impoverished, and

---

[2] Patrick Seger. "The Power of Hope." *Samaritan's Purse*, 24 Dec. 2013, www.samaritanspurse.org/article/the-power-of-hope.
[3] Jeffrey Kluger. "How Hope Works." *TIME.Com*, 7 Mar. 2013, healthland.time.com/2013/03/07/this-is-your-mind-on-hope.
[4] ibid
[5] Nicholas Kristof. "Opinion | The Power of Hope Is Real." *The New York Times*, 21 May 2015, www.nytimes.com/2015/05/21/opinion/nicholas-kristof-the-power-of-hope-is-real.html.

hopeless can have their lives turned around when they are given hope. While Karl Marx, one of the founders of the communist movement, once declared that "religion is the opiate [depressant] of the people," these studies found quite the opposite ... that religion—a hope-filled religion—is the amphetamine [stimulant] of the people! At the end of the extensive study, they discovered the one thing that works best to lift people out of extreme poverty: Not handouts, not money; rather, the power of hope.

These 21st Century writers, newspapers, magazines, and studies all serve to confirm what the Scriptures have told us for over 2000 years. Hope gives life. Hope carries us through suffering. In our journey, hope is coming to Job. His suffering has produced perseverance ... his perseverance, character ... and he is arriving at hope. He is no longer content to sit and mourn and merely (barely) exist. Something is rallying within him. Our faithful fellow is now becoming a hopeful fellow. This really is a journey for Job (perhaps for us) from one place in life to another.

A Faith of Hope

Hope is absolutely essential to the Christian faith. Jesus exuded hope in his message—Repent! Believe! Change! The kingdom of heaven, God's reign, the year of the Lord's favor is here, and you are about to see some crazy-amazing stuff! (Matt.2:17, Mark 1:15, Luke 4:18-19, John 1:50-51).

Paul brought things home nicely at the end of his section on 'love' in the letter to the Corinthian church: "And now these three remain: faith, hope and love" (I Cor.13:13a).

Hope is all over the New Testament (83 mentions), and hope needs to be all over our lives as Christians. When we bring our Christian faith to this understanding of hope, we find that biblical hope is *a deliberate process that recognizes where one is; where one wants or needs to be or where God wants us to be, is calling us to be; and a willingness to take the steps to get from the one place to the other.*

We see this in the unrelenting, repeating themes in the lives of the 'heroes of faith' and all through the Bible. Adam and Eve, Abraham, Isaac, Jacob, David, Isaiah, and all the others follow this process—whether in their personal lives or in the greater narrative of the people of God. These all find themselves in dire situations (where one is), they imagine a different life or are called to a different life (where one wants to be), and they embrace the ways of God and take action in order to get to that life (willingness to take the steps.)

In a recent Bible study on Job at our church, one of the attendees, Rosalynn,[6] pointed out that hope as described above is more than mere thinking—hope is action. Hope is doing what it takes to get from point A to point B. If hope is indeed an action, then those three grand hallmarks of the Christian life that Paul mentions—faith, hope, and love—are all three about action.

Faith goes beyond mere intellectual assent; faith—in the Biblical sense—must be accompanied by action (see James 2:14-26). The Biblical understanding of faith is a belief in, confidence in, trust in someone or something that leads us to action.

And, love goes far beyond the mere emotions we tend to limit it to in Western culture. Just see Jesus' life (a life of love) and Paul's passage on love (I Cor.13:4-7), and we understand that biblical love is a way of acting. Jesus tells us very clearly, "Greater love has no one than this: to lay down one's life for one's friends" (John 15:13). Love is action. If love were a mere feeling, it would come and go with the wind as all feelings do. Love is acting in a particular way in spite of our feelings.

But let us stick with hope for now as we understand that hope, too, is something far beyond wishful thinking. Hope is a

---

[6] Name used with permission.

combination of seeing where we are, the situation we are in, seeing where we or God needs or wants us to be, and taking the necessary steps to get there. Of course, as Christians, we know that we cannot always take those 'necessary steps' on our own. Much to the chagrin of many, Christianity is not a 'self-help,' 'pull-yourself-up-by-your-bootstraps' thing. We know we need God's help, God's Spirit, and the help of God's people (the Church) to become who God is shaping us to be.

Job is keenly aware that he is powerless before the events of his life. He could not stop the loss of his wealth, family, and health, and he cannot turn around his situation by wishing. He must hope—recognize where he is, he must see a different way of being and he must take the first step—crying out to God.

Jesus is our author of hope. If hope is a deliberate process that recognizes where one is, where one wants or needs to be, and a willingness to take the steps to get from one place to the other, who reveals this better or more clearly than Jesus in the Gospels? At the heart of the proclamation of the Good News of God's Kingdom (Matt. 4:17, Mk. 1:15, Luke 4:43, John 3:3ff) we hear the message of hope, the possibility of change, a call for renewal. Where would we Christians be and who would we be today if not for the hopeful, life-changing faith that God gives us in Christ Jesus?

Jesus' call to repentance—"the kingdom of God is at hand; repent and believe in the gospel"—is a call of hope: we can change our way of thinking and direction of our lives. To repent simply means to turn from going in one direction to going in another. Jesus would not call us to do something we could not do. With God's help, we can change the direction of our lives!

Jesus' call to discipleship—"Deny yourself, take up your cross, and follow me"—is a call of hope: we can live differently by learning from Jesus. Disciple-life is a life walking in Jesus' steps, following him, living like him. Jesus would not call us to this life if it were something inaccessible, something we could not do. With God's help, we can begin living the disciple life.

Jesus' call to mission—"Go therefore into all the world...." and "you will be my witnesses"—is a call of hope—we can change the world as God's people, with God's help. Jesus sees a new reality, a kingdom-of-God reality that can happen when we who are Christians, we who are the Church, recognize where we are and where we need to be in the world, and we then take steps in that direction. With God's help, working together, we can change the world.

Christians are presumed to be a people of hope. Peter writes, "Always be prepared to give an answer to everyone who asks you to give the reason for the hope that you have" (I Peter 3:15). Peter knows that the world is watching us, and he knows that they will see the hope we have in our lives (if we are living faithfully, trustingly, believingly), and they are going to ask us how we can be a people of hope in the brokenness of this world, in the reality of suffering. How will we answer them?

On the Journey through Suffering—

So, where has this journey with Job taken us? We see that even in the midst of suffering, even when we feel we or the ones we love may have lost everything, there is still a place for hope. In fact, Paul reminds us that hope grows out of suffering: We see where we are; we see where we need or want to be, or where God calls us to be; we determine to trust God's work in us and to do whatever is necessary to get from point A to point B—and that is hope in action.

As Christians living three or four thousand years after Job, we now know two of the greatest things we can do as followers of Jesus: 1) Hold on to the hope within our own lives; 2) Sow seeds of hope in the lives of others—help them to see that our God is a God of change, that change is possible. Rather than be like Job's friends, we are not stuck wherever we might be. Our friends and loved ones are not stuck.

My friend, Marjan, was in a dark place at the beginning of our conversations in early 2021. Everything seemed uncertain and unknown ... with good reason. Today, she has dreams again. She is beginning to look forward to what lies ahead of her in the months and years to come. Suffering has produced character, perseverance ... and hope. She is starting to see possibilities related to work and school and life. These dreams and anticipations are products of the embers of hope that begin to glow within her.

Perhaps our reading of Job has shown you where you are (or where you were) and has given you a desire or a sense of call to be somewhere else, to be someone else, to see the world differently. Now is the time to lay hold of hope, to plan the next step, and step out. This is hope.

Questions for Reflection—

1. In a time of suffering in your life, have you experienced a shift from hopelessness to hope?

_____
_____
_____

2. Have you seen the power of hope work in others' lives?

_____
_____
_____

3. After reading this chapter, has your understanding of 'hope' changed in any way? How?

_____
_____
_____

Chapter 8
JOB QUESTIONS REALITY
JOB 15 – 31

In these intervening chapters, we find no less than 62 questions asked—some spoken by the friends to Job, some by Job to the friends, some asked to God; some are rhetorical, and some are seeking real answers. Perhaps we, too, have questions about suffering, about the injustice in this world, and perhaps we are waiting for answers as well.

Writer and poet, Aviya Kushner, points out the following:

> "In the beginning, the Bible presents God as the asker of questions. In the Garden of Eden, God asks Adam, 'Where are you?' God asks Cain a version of the same question—'Where is your brother?' And then, as the Bible continues, the situation flips. Man asks God questions. Job confronts God; Isaiah has some tough questions for God ... we were no longer answering questions about God ... we, too, found ourselves asking God where he was." [1]

Yes, Job 15-31 ask lots of questions—lots! And, in the middle of all of these questions, in Job 21, we realize through his questions and

---

[1] Aviya Kushner. *The Grammar of God: A Journey into the Words and Worlds of the Bible*. (First Edition, Random House, 2015) 154.

declarations that Job the man reaches another turning point on his journey. In this chapter, we see clearly that Job has reached his limit with his friends. *Enough!* He is not going to put up with this 'blither and blather' that his friends have been spewing now for too many chapters.

Where is the Justice?

Job begins this chapter getting his friends' attention, and then he points out the very obvious:

> 2"Listen carefully to my words;
>   let this be the consolation you give me.
> 3Bear with me while I speak,
>   and after I have spoken, mock on.
> 4"Is my complaint directed to a human being?
>   Why should I not be impatient?
> 5Look at me and be appalled;
>   clap your hand over your mouth.
> 6When I think about this, I am terrified;
>   trembling seizes my body.
> 7Why do the wicked live on,
>   growing old and increasing in power?
> 8They see their children established around them,
>   their offspring before their eyes.
> 9Their homes are safe and free from fear;
>   the rod of God is not on them.
> 10Their bulls never fail to breed;
>   their cows calve and do not miscarry.
> 11They send forth their children as a flock;
>   their little ones dance about.
> 12They sing to the music of timbrel and lyre;
>   they make merry to the sound of the pipe.
> 13They spend their years in prosperity

and go down to the grave in peace.
[14]Yet they say to God, 'Leave us alone!
We have no desire to know your ways.
[15]Who is the Almighty, that we should serve him?
What would we gain by praying to him?'
[16]But their prosperity is not in their own hands,
so I stand aloof from the plans of the wicked.
[17]"Yet how often is the lamp of the wicked snuffed out?
How often does calamity come upon them,
the fate God allots in his anger?
[18]How often are they like straw before the wind,
like chaff swept away by a gale?
[19]It is said, 'God stores up the punishment of the wicked for their children.'
Let him repay the wicked, so that they themselves will experience it!   (Job 21:2-19)

Job basically says to his friends, "If everything you say is true, why isn't it actually happening?! If 'God stores up the punishment of the wicked for their children' (v.19), then why are so many of them living large and having the time of their lives?"

We have asked the same question. And, we have asked that question because on some level we believe that this world should operate on 'karma,' that everyone should 'get what's coming to them.' Yet, we see that this does not happen.

We see rotten politicians staying in power, gaining more wealth and power. We see our 'godless' neighbor doing yet another renovation on his house and yard so he has a place to park his new boat and his new SUV. We see that self-important, arrogant woman who is on husband #4, who has spent thousands on nips and tucks and enhancements ... and she looks stunning and seems to be really enjoying the high life. And we who strive to live simple, godly lives cry out (in jealously, perhaps!), "Where is the justice? Where is the anger of God against these people? When will they have their Job moment and lose it all?!"

I was in seminary enrolled in the History of Methodism. The instructor was a good-hearted man but a bit too trusting, in my humble opinion. The end of the semester came, and I was sitting on an A/B borderline grade. If I got an 'A' on the final, I would have an 'A' in the class, and if I got a 'B', then a 'B' in the class. The final exam was a take-home exam—but the instructions were very clear: we were to study first, put away our notes and books, and then take the test (not an open-book test). That is what I did—I did as I was directed. I followed orders. I was one of the few students in the class to do as directed, and I later discovered I was one of the few in the class to get a 'B' on the exam. That 'B' kept me from graduating with honors.

I prayed for God's vengeance on those sorry, pastor-wanna-be students around me! Like Job, I cried out, "Let God repay the wicked!" They, too, graduated—some of them with honors. (I am still just a little sore about that event some 24 years later.) I wanted vengeance! Where was the justice?

We have read about and heard about the vengeance of God, the justice of God. Our problem is that we want to decide how and when and to whom God directs that vengeance and justice. And, as we mentioned earlier, we are quick to wish that vengeance towards those who offend us, who offend those we love, who offend our place or our nation. Funny, however, when it comes to our own missteps, mistakes, and sins, how we deftly deflect any need for God to direct vengeance at us. Someone offends us, and we cry, "Justice!" When we are the offenders, we cry, "Mercy!"

Scripture solves this problem for us. In the New Testament, we see the disciples wanting to direct that same vengeance and justice of God at those who offend them:

> ⁵²And [Jesus] sent messengers on ahead, who went into a Samaritan village to get things ready for him; ⁵³but the people there did not welcome him, because he was heading for Jerusalem. ⁵⁴When the disciples James and John saw this, they asked, "Lord, do you want us to call fire down from heaven to destroy them?" (Luke 9:52-54)

"Call down fire from heaven"? Really? I guess the disciples were tired. They just wanted to rest and relax, and they were offended by the rejection of these folks. Yet, I wonder if the people might have had the same reaction towards the disciples when the disciples rejected them?

> Then people brought little children to Jesus for him to place his hands on them and pray for them. But the disciples rebuked them. (Matthew 9:13)

Did some of those parents think, "God, hit these guys where it hurts! I want my child blessed!"?

Well, in both cases, Jesus was having none of it. He called the children to himself, and he had the disciples relent on their desire to bring vengeance on the Samaritan village— "But Jesus turned and rebuked [his disciples]. Then he and his disciples went to another village" (v.55-56).

Paul finally articulates clearly what we find in the actions and words of Jesus. Actually, he reaches back into the history and tradition of God's people and reminds them of something they already know—or should know:

> "Do not take revenge, my dear friends, but leave room for God's wrath, for it is written: 'It is mine to avenge; I will repay,' says the Lord" (Romans 12:19).

Paul counsels the Christians in Rome who are suffering the ire of both the established Jewish community and the Roman officials by reminding them of God's promise found in Deuteronomy 32:35.

Though they were suffering unjustly, though perhaps they were angry about their suffering, God would take care of things.

We do not have to worry about justice. Oh, yes, we continue to strive for justice (Isaiah 1:17), we work for justice (Micah 6:8), we demand justice (Amos 5:24), but we cannot force justice. We do not have the power to direct God's vengeance ("wrath"). We do what we can to bring about justice within the bounds of Christian love, and then we trust God to do what is right, when it is right, to whom it is right (this is the 'faith' part of "faith, hope, and love"). We rest in God's goodness, in God's unchanging character, and in God's decisions of what, when, and to whom God should do things.

Job finally realizes and articulates the reality of the situation. The wicked prosper. He—a righteous person—is suffering. That old way of seeing things, the worldview that has sustained him for so long is no longer holding water. The 'retribution principle' no longer explains the reality he sees around him. And, I hope that we, too, can let go of this idea that those who do 'right' prosper and those who do 'wrong' suffer. This idea was not the actual reality of Job's world, and this is certainly not the reality of our world.

On the Journey through Suffering—

The good news here is that Job is coming around! He is finally seeing things as they really are, not as his friends insist, not—perhaps—as he once did. His journey through suffering is helping him understand that he did not see things clearly, that he has much to learn.

I wondered if Marjan was seeing things as I have suggested. Did she recognize that our world is broken, and that 'bad things happen to good people' just as 'good things happen to bad people'? Did she see this place as a 'broken world' where some suffer more and some less?

To cease my wondering, I called her and asked her: Why do you think bad things happen to good people and good things to bad people, and why did this cancer happen to you? Her response:

> Bad things happen to everyone. It is really random—no reason to what happens in this world. There is no way to prevent the bad things that happen. There was another woman the same age me with the same cancer I had. She is gone. For some reason, the chemo worked 100% in me and not at all in her.
>
> I've asked the question a lot—why did this happen to me? I wanted there to be a reason. I was hoping there was a reason, and I was hoping for an answer.
>
> I saw a film recently. There was an illness situation similar to mine, and the character was so angry. Another character pointed out, 'If you are angry, you must believe there is a power that could prevent this or caused this. You must believe something is broken.' I was angry, so I suppose deep down I wanted to believe there was a reason, and I wanted to believe something or someone would fix everything.
>
> But, now, I'm thinking the world is just the way the world is. It is what it is. If there is a God, why did he not help me? If there is a God, why are there so many things wrong in the world? If God and Lucifer are fighting, why do I have to suffer?

Marjan does not have all of the answers to her questions, but she does have good questions.

Our journey with Job reveals that suffering in our lives is a result of the powers of evil determined to shake our faith in God, is a result of our actions and the actions of others all related to our free-will, or is a result of living in a sin-broken world where things have gotten terribly off track from God's original design.

Marjan's observation about our anger at the situation being a sign of belief—that is intriguing. I will think more on that, but there seems to be a validity there. If we did not presume a cause outside of the natural order of things or presume the existence of a power that could change the situation, why get angry? And, if this is true, then we do know—from our journey with Job—that there are causes of suffering in our world outside the natural order and a power than can change the situation.

May what we are encountering in this journey help us see that we, too, can change our way of thinking. May God help us to see the world differently—as the world is seen from God's perspective, as it is understood from a biblical perspective. May we see where suffering comes from. May we comfort and be comforted in times of suffering. May we latch on to hope. May we trust in God's grace and wisdom if we suffer from injustice. These are the places Job is taking us as we journey forward.

Questions for Reflection—

1. Have you experienced injustice? What was the situation, and how did you react?

_____
_____
_____

2. Have you dealt with others unjustly or unfairly? What was the situation, and how did you respond when you realized you were acting unjustly or unfairly?

_____
_____

3. Like Marjan, have you wondered at times why God does not take action to end suffering—your and others?

_____
_____
_____

Chapter 9
JOB BEGINS TO UNDERSTAND
JOB 31:35-37

We are making our way through the book of Job, and we are approaching the end of this journey with Job—an interesting journey to be sure! As we get towards the end, let us take a moment to look back on what we have learned from Job about suffering:

- Suffering is common to all of us as people, though in various forms.
- Suffering is not from God; it is from Satan, bad or evil decisions (ours and others'), and/or a broken world.
- Suffering is more bearable when we share the pain with others, with friends.
- Suffering may be a good time to talk to the sufferer about God; it is always a good time to talk to God about the one suffering: Pray for those who suffer.
- Suffering can and should be articulated—we can scream, yell, weep, and wail. There is a place for lament.
- Suffering can bring us closer to God; suffering can open our ears to hear God.
- Suffering produces perseverance, character and, ultimately, hope!

- Suffering because of injustice may or may not be something we can set right (we should strive for justice), but we know God can and will—in God's time, in God's way.

Let us continue our journey with the man called Job through this fascinating book. In the reading below, Job cries out to God for justice, for an answer.

Job Turns a Corner

Job speaks:

> ³⁵"Oh, that I had someone to hear me!
> I sign now my defense—let the Almighty answer me;
> let my accuser put his indictment in writing.
> ³⁶Surely I would wear it on my shoulder,
> I would put it on like a crown.
> ³⁷I would give him an account of my every step;
> I would present it to him as to a ruler. (Job 31:35-37)

Job is frustrated. His friends keep telling him that his suffering is a product of his own sin, that he has somehow offended God. Job has examined his life, looked at it from every angle, turned it upside-down, but he cannot find this supposed offense—certainly nothing to merit this degree of suffering. He is a man of integrity—if he found the sin in his life, he would name it, own it. But, he can find nothing. Is he still operating from his friends' perspective—God rewards the good and punishes the bad?

Job is about to learn what Jesus' disciples learned from their Master some 2000 years later. The world is not set up on this good/bad = reward/punishment scale. In fact, if we were to really and truly think about it, would we even want things to work this way? Do we really want the world to function according to this law of cause and effect?

Oh, it is so easy to want it when we see violence and injustice around us, but do we want God to deal with us personally this way? Do I really want God to step in and deal out punishment and suffering on me every time I think and act selfishly? Do I really want to suffer every time I short-cut the law through some "if-y" loophole? Do I want God to send fire and desert winds on me when I arrogantly think myself better than those around me? Do I want God to pin me down with illness and rob me of family and income because I have committed a sin against God or someone else? No way! When it comes to me, I want grace, pardon, forgiveness. I only want that retribution principle, that 'law of karma,' to go into effect when someone sins against me, mine, or my world.

Job is where he is. He makes his case before God. He refutes his guilt. Listen to Job's words from the same chapter:

> 5"If I have walked with falsehood
>   or my foot has hurried after deceit—...
> 9"If my heart has been enticed by a woman,
>   or if I have lurked at my neighbor's door...
> 13"If I have denied justice to any of my servants,
>   whether male or female, when they had a
>   grievance against me...
> 16"If I have denied the desires of the poor
>   or let the eyes of the widow grow weary...
> 24"If I have put my trust in gold
>   or said to pure gold, 'You are my security'...
> 29"If I have rejoiced at my enemy's misfortune
>   or gloated over the trouble that came to him....
> (Job 31:5-29)

If, if, if...if I had done any of these things, God would have a right to punish me, but I am blameless! says Job.

So, what is going on?!?

This brings us to Job's cry: "Oh, that I had someone to hear me! I sign now my defense—let the Almighty answer me... (Job 31:35).

And God does.

God Answers Job

Let us hear what God has to say:

> ¹Then the LORD spoke to Job out of the storm. He said:
> ²"Who is this that obscures my plans
>   with words without knowledge?
> ³Brace yourself like a man;
>   I will question you,
>   and you shall answer me.
> ⁴"Where were you when I laid the earth's foundation?
>   Tell me, if you understand.
> ⁵Who marked off its dimensions? Surely you know!
>   Who stretched a measuring line across it?
> ⁶On what were its footings set,
>   or who laid its cornerstone—
> ⁷while the morning stars sang together
>   and all the angels shouted for joy?
> ⁸"Who shut up the sea behind doors
>   when it burst forth from the womb,
> ⁹when I made the clouds its garment
>   and wrapped it in thick darkness,
> ¹⁰when I fixed limits for it
>   and set its doors and bars in place,
> ¹¹when I said, 'This far you may come and no farther;
>   here is where your proud waves halt'?
> ³¹"Can you bind the chains of the Pleiades?
>   Can you loosen Orion's belt?
> ³²Can you bring forth the constellations in their

>   seasons or lead out the Bear with its cubs?
> ³³Do you know the laws of the heavens?
>   Can you set up God's dominion over the earth?
> ³⁴"Can you raise your voice to the clouds
>   and cover yourself with a flood of water?
> ³⁵Do you send the lightning bolts on their way?
>   Do they report to you, 'Here we are'?
> ³⁶Who gives the ibis wisdom
>   or gives the rooster understanding?
> ³⁷Who has the wisdom to count the clouds?
>   Who can tip over the water jars of the heavens
> ³⁸when the dust becomes hard
>   and the clods of earth stick together?
> ³⁹"Do you hunt the prey for the lioness
>   and satisfy the hunger of the lions
> ⁴⁰when they crouch in their dens
>   or lie in wait in a thicket?
> ⁴¹Who provides food for the raven
>   when its young cry out to God
>   (Job 38:1-11; 31-41)

As I read these words, I am reminded of what God says through Isaiah:

> "For my thoughts are not your thoughts, neither are your ways my ways," declares the LORD. "As the heavens are higher than the earth, so are my ways higher than your ways and my thoughts than your thoughts."
>   (Isaiah 55:8-9)

Job (and we!) has no clue about the greatness, the power, of God. Job and we are mere specks of dust on the face of one of one billion balls of rock floating in a universe that we barely understand. Oh, scientists make out like they know so much (and they are learning a lot—but their 'a lot' is but a scratch on the surface, I imagine), and much of it is guess-work and hope and good intention. But does anyone really know where we have come from, how we hold together, and where we are going? Our best and brightest scientists talk about a "Big Bang," but few of them offer any speculation about what caused that 'bang' or why all the matter of the universe was gathered in one place or how it came to be there. Their ideas only go back so far, but our God goes back even farther.

This passage in Job 38 also reveals God's interests, God's areas of concern. Perhaps surprising to Job and some readers here, we see clearly that God cares for all of creation. God is interested in the earth, the oceans, the mountains, the rivers. God is concerned about the lions, the ravens, the horses, the eagles. And God is concerned about people as well. God is the Creator, so this should not come as a surprise.

Who is this God? Thankfully, in these words from God found here in Job, an image of the Creator and Sustainer of all things emerges. God is Maker, Giver, Builder and Provider ... not destroyer, killer, and 'unmaker.'

Jesus—Image of God

Jump with me to the New Testament for a moment. The apostle Paul has some very important words for us as we strive to get this image of God into our minds. In fact, Paul provides us with another foundational doctrine and belief of the Christian faith.

In his letter to the Christians in the city of Colossae, Paul writes these words as he strives to help them understand more about both God and Jesus Christ:

> The Son is the image of the invisible God, the firstborn over all creation. For in him all things were created: things in heaven and on earth, visible and invisible, whether thrones or powers or rulers or authorities; all

things have been created through him and for him. He is before all things, and in him all things hold together. And he is the head of the body, the church; he is the beginning and the firstborn from among the dead, so that in everything he might have the supremacy. For God was pleased to have all his fullness dwell in him, and through him to reconcile to himself all things, whether things on earth or things in heaven, by making peace through his blood, shed on the cross.
(Colossians 1:15-20)

According to Paul, according to Scripture, according to orthodox Christian theology, God is exactly who we find in the Son, Jesus Christ. In other words, if we want to have an inkling of who the transcendent Creator God is, we need to look at Jesus. Jesus is the "image of the invisible God;" God's "fullness" dwells in Jesus. To see and know Jesus is to see and know God. Jesus heals. Jesus restores. Jesus provides. The pain and destruction we see happening in Job is not something we could conceive of coming from Jesus.

When we think of Jesus, when we see Jesus in the Gospels, what do we find there? Do we find a destroyer? A killer? A peddler of suffering and pain? An unmaker?

James provides us another piece of the puzzle: "Every good and perfect gift is from above, coming down from the Father of the heavenly lights, who does not change" (James 1:17). God is the source of all that is good and perfect, and God does not change from being that.

In Jesus we find a maker, a healer, a restorer, a guide, a teacher, a friend ... a source of goodness. He has opportunities throughout his ministry to act out that law of retribution, of good/bad = reward/punishment. He has plenty of chances to bring suffering to the evil and bad people who surely roam the roads and villages of 1st Century Judea. But, no. He could have called down armies of angels to deal with those who meted out injustice. But, no. He could have just as easily cast disease on the evil people. But, no.

In the following passage from the Gospels, we get a glimpse of God and the ways of God:

> 43"You have heard that it was said, 'Love your neighbor and hate your enemy.' 44But I tell you, love your enemies and pray for those who persecute you, 45that you may be children of your Father in heaven. He causes his sun to rise on the evil and the good, and sends rain on the righteous and the unrighteous. 46If you love those who love you, what reward will you get? Are not even the tax collectors doing that? 47And if you greet only your own people, what are you doing more than others? Do not even pagans do that? 48Be perfect, therefore, as your heavenly Father is perfect. (Matt. 5:43-48)

Jesus here gives us his own understanding of the ways of God. Rather than seeing a God of retribution and 'tit-for-tat', Jesus reveals a God who would have us 'love your enemies and pray for those who persecute you.' God is one who shares good and blessings with all regardless of their goodness or righteousness (right-ness). And, not only is God like this, Jesus calls us to be like this as well!

One and the Same God

As we began this study, we affirmed our belief in the sovereignty of God. Today, let us also affirm our belief in the unchanging nature of God's character. If that is so, and if Jesus is the image of God, then the God we see in Jesus is the same God we find in the book of Job. Jesus is maker, healer, giver, provider—the image of the invisible God. And that image of God reveals a 'good' God.

In fact, when we look at the New Testament, we find Jesus going throughout the land touching lives. He heals the sick, makes the lame to walk, drives demons from the possessed, and even raises three people to life. If suffering is from God, then Jesus is working in direct opposition to God in all of his ministry. Read the previous sentence again. If these situations of people's lives (suffering) are "the will of God," then Jesus is acting in direct contradiction to the will of God. Of course, Jesus—by nature—cannot be working in opposition to God. Therefore, we are again assured that illness and suffering and death are not something from God. Jesus works to undo the work of evil, the brokenness of this world, the effects of Godless actions and selfish attitudes.

If Jesus is the image of the invisible God as Paul declares and orthodox, Christian theology affirms, let us imagine, then, that Jesus is God. Let us apply this simple theological truth to the more widely-held understanding of blessing and cursing we hear from far too many people who call themselves Christians. How does it sound to say or even think the following?

"Yeah, I lost my job. Must be Jesus' will..."

"Jesus always takes the best first..."

"Yes, I've got cancer. I just need to accept Jesus' will, that Jesus wants me sick right now...."

"Our business was destroyed in the hurricane. Jesus knows what he's doing."

We recoil in horror at such ideas! Unless you are a rather unusual person, neither you nor I could ever imagine saying anything like that nor could we accuse Jesus of having a hand in such things. The Jesus we see in the Gospels is Jesus the Son of God, "the image of the invisible God." So, if we are willing to say God would do it, we must be ready to say that Jesus would do it, too.

And we are not ready to say those sorts of things about Jesus—I pray! Jesus is good. And God is good—all the time.

Social media often float those lists of characteristics of people, sort of like the old "You're a redneck if...." Recently I saw one about Methodists on Facebook. One of the commonalities among Methodists is our recognition of the goodness of God (another is our affinity for 'church suppers'—"How can you tell the difference between a Baptist and Methodist walking to church? The Baptist carries a Bible, and the Methodist carries a casserole."). That recognition of God's goodness is often captured in a little practice common in many of our churches. The pastor or worship leader calls out, "God is good!" and the people respond, "All the time!"

Have you done this in your congregation? This is a time of affirmation ... affirming a truth of God that we find in Jesus, of God who we find in in the book of Job:

"God is good…all the time; all the time…God is good!"

This is not only a fun to practice in our congregations and small groups, but it also reveals a truth we need to lay hold of, a truth we need to really grasp and internalize. When we see Jesus, we know God's goodness is true. If God's goodness is true (as we believe it is), Job's suffering has not and cannot come from God. Job is learning that God's goodness is true, and I pray that we are grasping this truth as we walk along with Job on this journey.

On the Journey through Suffering—

My friends, we have got to latch on to this idea: the Goodness of God. We cannot be led astray by Satan, by bad theologies, by well-intentioned but misguided teachings. Our God is good. God is maker, builder, sustainer, provider.

As we go into the days ahead—in the struggles we may face with school traffic tomorrow morning; teachers, in the frustrations that you encounter in the classrooms this week; students, during the difficulties you face in the classrooms this week or this semester;

parents, the trouble you have getting those kiddos out the door each morning; working men and women, in the day-to-day challenges you face in the work place and on the work-site; husbands and wives, on the roller-coaster experiences in your relationships; for all, in the pain and suffering of illness or loss or injury—as we go into days ahead, let us face the hardships with 'clear eyes' knowing that God is not the source of our problems. Rather, God is the answer to our problems ... because God is good (All the Time!) ... and all the time (God is good!)

When we face the trials, struggles, tensions, and sufferings that come to us this week, this month, this year, claim the truth: God is good ... all the time. When we get confused as to who is causing what in our lives or in the world, and we get turned around like Job, thinking the bad stuff is from God, let us stop, take a breath, and claim the truth: God is Good ... all the time. If something is not good, it is not from God. Let us not accuse God of those things 'not good' in our lives. Let us remember that our good God goes with us, hears us, strengthens us ... and never forsakes us.

I was curious as to what Marjan sensed about God. She knew I was a minister, and we had talked about God in some general ways through her chemotherapy. But, I wanted to know what she thought of God, what sense she had of God.

I asked Marjan: How is God perceived in your culture (Iranian/Persian), and what is your own sense of God?

> My culture in Iran is mostly Shiite Muslim. Most Iranian Muslims believe there is a heaven and a hell. The good people will go to heaven and the bad people will go to hell (sounds just like the world of Job and the 'retribution principle'!). If you asked the average person on the street what they think of God, they will say, 'God is kind,' but, they say that out of fear because they believe that God is

vengeful and judgmental. So, they don't want to say anything to make God angry.

What do I think of God? I don't know. I don't care right now. But, I still get angry sometimes about my situation. So, maybe I do believe a little?

What a different view of God from that of our culture. Not that our culture in the West has a clear or biblical view of God. Too often, the western European/North American view is that of a Deist God (the distant, detached 'watchmaker') or, in the United States, God becomes inextricably wound up in patriotic rhetoric—things become very confusing.

Our journey with Job is showing us that God is 'good.' Good to us in our suffering. Good to us in a thousand small ways that we may not be aware of or do not acknowledge. But God is good. This, my friends, is a big part of God's Good News for us.

Questions for Reflection—

1. Have you—like many—seen the "Old Testament God" different and distinct from the "New Testament God"? Does it help to reconcile the two images in Jesus?

_____
_____
_____

2. When have you inadvertently accused God of doing something "bad"? Can you see now that the "bad" was not from God?

_____
_____

3. Marjan talks of people who speak nicely about God out of fear. Do you fear God in this way? How do you respond if someone asks you about the nature of God?

_____
_____
_____

Chapter 10
GOD SPEAKS AND JOB LISTENS...AND LEARNS
JOB 41:1-11

From early on in the book of Job (chap. 4), the man Job has called out to God to respond, to speak, and in Job 38, God begins to speak. Why would God wait so long to respond? Or, does it just seem like a long time to us—to our generation so accustomed to instant messaging, instant coffee, and same-day delivery from our favorite on-line super-store? Yet, before we dive into God's response, there is one other issue we need to address.

We have learned much about suffering in this world, but I have been amiss. I have not yet really defined "suffering." We have been kicking around the word as though its meaning is clear to all. But, from my years of teaching and preaching, I know that the best thing to do is provide a definition for us to work with. Here we go.

What is "Suffering"?

We have a tendency to label anything and everything that hurts, or that runs contrary to our will and desire, as suffering, but that is not so. Not everything that 'hurts' is suffering. We have many things in this world that cause pain—some of the pain is short-term, some of it longer-term. Yet, not all of the pains in this life are "suffering." Discomfort is not the same as suffering.

The young men and women in grade school and university who go out for football, basketball, cheerleading, softball, marching band, color-guard, and any other similar physically demanding extra-curricular activity—all of these know what it means to hurt, to experience pain, to endure discomfort as they put in hours of practice in the hot sun, too early in the morning, too late at night ... but we would not really label any of these as 'suffering.'

Mission teams serving in cross-cultural settings experience heat or cold, strange foods, puzzling difficulties, sleepless nights, 'Montezuma's Revenge,' and any number of other unpleasantries. In the congregation I serve now, teams go out to build access ramps for homes of disabled folk. The weather at times is so hot in south Texas--110°F. Boards are heavy. Splinters are shared by all. But neither for the international mission teams nor the local work teams would we call the experiences 'suffering.'

There are times we engage in self-improvement—aerobics, weightlifting, running, continuing education, community service, etc.—and while these forms of exercise or involvement may include or result in pain and discomfort, we would not label any of these as 'suffering.'

Being disciplined (punished, corrected) in and of itself is not suffering. As parents—unless we want a house full of hellions—we must tell our children 'no,' we must correct their behavior through both positive (Yay! Good job!) and negative (perhaps a 'smack!' on the hand ... or elsewhere) reinforcement, but in normal, healthy situations, we would not say that the children are suffering when they are simply being appropriately disciplined. There are indications in Scripture that God disciplines us (see Hebrews 12:4-11), but 'discipline' and 'cause to suffer' are (should be!) two different things.

So, what is suffering? How do we understand suffering? Here is a working definition for us, a definition I have compiled after reviewing the definitions of various dictionaries and encyclopedias, and after experiences and conversations regarding this theme:

> Suffering is enduring, going through, or experiencing prolonged physical, mental and/or emotional pain as a result of illness, injury and/or loss.

The crucial words here in the definition of suffering are *enduring*, *prolonged*, and *pain*. Without a doubt, when we look at Job's life, we clearly see suffering as defined here.

In my childhood, my dog, Tippy, was hit while crossing a busy highway. He sustained injury—it hurt, I am sure—but he died almost instantly. My father remarked at the time, probably to console me, "Well, at least he didn't suffer."

One of my parishioners recently lost his mother. She had been diagnosed with cancer four years before and had undergone almost three years of chemotherapy. When she passed recently, he remarked, "At least the suffering is over...." She did suffer. Suffering is about enduring prolonged pain. Many of us really do understand what it means to suffer.

When I was serving the Chicopee parish in north Georgia, I took our daughters, Jesse and Megan, ice skating one afternoon. I am not a great skater, but I can get going. Stopping? Well, I am not so good at that. As I was coming around the corner and picking up speed for the straightaway, two small boys jumped into the rink in front of me without looking. I am 6'3", 175 lbs, and I was traveling about 10-15 miles an hour. If I had hit them, I would have hurt them. In my flailing, clumsy way, I immediately tried to stop. The tip of my skate grabbed the ice. My knee traveled in a new direction. There was a loud "pop." I came to rest sprawled on the ice. The boys never even saw me.

For years, my knee would hurt if I did any kind of strenuous exercise. I even decided to give up driving a manual transmission car (fun!) because my left knee would begin to ache if I had to drive in stop-and-go traffic. Even today if I take an especially long hike, the pain returns to remind me of that ice-skating accident. I have learned through the years what suffering is: prolonged physical, mental and/or emotional pain as a result of illness, injury and/or loss. Let me point out that my suffering was not caused by God, by evil, or by my bad choices. I suffered for the ignorance of young children who did not know they were putting themselves in danger.

Now, with a clear definition of suffering in hand, let us see how God responds to Job's challenges.

God Speaks

We join the story and resume the journey once again as God is talking to Job, answering Job's challenge from chapter 31:

> [The LORD continued,]
> ¹"Can you pull in Leviathan with a fishhook
>   or tie down its tongue with a rope?
> ²Can you put a cord through its nose
>   or pierce its jaw with a hook?
> ³Will it keep begging you for mercy?
>   Will it speak to you with gentle words?
> ⁴Will it make an agreement with you
>   for you to take it as your slave for life?
> ⁵Can you make a pet of it like a bird
>   or put it on a leash for the young women in your house?
> ⁶Will traders barter for it?
>   Will they divide it up among the merchants?
> ⁷Can you fill its hide with harpoons
>   or its head with fishing spears?
> ⁸If you lay a hand on it,

you will remember the struggle and never do it
   again!
⁹Any hope of subduing it is false;
   the mere sight of it is overpowering.
¹⁰No one is fierce enough to rouse it.
   Who then is able to stand against me?
¹¹Who has a claim against me that I must pay?
   Everything under heaven belongs to me.
                    (Job 41:1-11)

This passage, as do earlier passages (I do hope you take time to read Job all the way though some time), reveals God's power. Yet, God reveals more than power.

Interestingly, God never demeans or denigrates Job or humanity in general. He says and indicates things like, "You don't understand; you don't see it all"…and, "You're not the center of the world, the only thing I care about." But, we never hear God saying things like, "You're a dunce! You don't matter; you're useless." In all of this—in the face of the foolishness of humanity—God does not condemn the man for his ignorance. Rather, like a good Father (an image Jesus insists on in the New Testament), God strives to help Job see the truth of reality in a way he can understand it.

If anyone exemplifies patience in the book of Job, it is God. By the time we arrive at this point in the journey, we discover that Job is more faithful than patient. We should know Job for his faithfulness in the face of diversity. God, on the other hand, is the patient One. God's patience through all of this is rather amazing—patient with Satan who comes again and again, patient with the friends and their erroneous advice, and patient with Job who is slow to understand that he simply does not understand what is going on and how the world works. And, if we have any doubt, we can look at our own lives and know that God's patience is surpassed only by His love for us. Has God not been patient with us?

Leviathan? Scholars are not in agreement, but it seems to be some monstrous sea creature from some uncertain time. We do not really know what creature this is, but we get it—this is some creature with seemingly unstoppable, untamable power, something that everyone fears and dreads. Yet, in the end, this powerful beast, this symbol of all things frightening to humankind, is simply another part of God's creation under God's power. God declares, "Everything under heaven belongs to me."

What source of suffering in our own lives seems 'unstoppable'? What 'leviathan' seems to threaten our lives and our dreams and goals, or the dreams and goals of those we love who suffer? God whispers to us, "Everything under heaven belongs to me." What person or situation in our lives seems like an untamable beast? God reminds us, "Everything under heaven belongs to me."

Job's Response

Job responds to the Almighty:

> ¹Then Job responded to the LORD:
> ²"I know that you can do all things;
>   Your intentions can not be thwarted.
> ³You asked, 'Who is this that questions my plans
>   with no real knowledge?'
>   I admit it—I spoke of things I had no clue about,
>   things so far beyond me.
> ⁴"You said, 'Listen, my turn;
>   I'll quiz you, and you'll answer me.'
> ⁵I had always heard of you
>   but now I have seen you—
>   you have shown me reality.
> ⁶Therefore I am nothing
>   and repent of dust and ashes."
>
> (Job 42:1-6, author's paraphrase)

Finally, Job gets it: God is God, and Job is not. There are things too wonderful to understand. God has a whole lot more going on than we see on the surface. Too often, we presume we are the center of the universe, that everything—even God's interests—revolve around us. God's reality is far bigger than ours. There is a mystery to life that we simply cannot see from this side of things.

God never explains to Job that Satan was the one who brought all the grief and pain to his life. God never explains God's self to anyone! But, God helps Job see that there is far more to what is going on than we see. And Job accepts it.

The final words of the passage above are awkward in the Hebrew—translated in different ways—but best rendered, I am convinced: "I repent of dust and ashes." *I am done sitting here. I can do no more sitting here feeling sorry for myself, and I'm not going to understand it all. Time to get up and move on.*

Back to Jesus—One More Time

Part of the problem in making sense of all this is that Job lives some 2000 years before Jesus, and we are reading this book of Job 2000 years after Jesus.

Job is doing the best he can in a pre-Christian world, in a world before Jesus, in a world before the Resurrection and the out-pouring of the Spirit of God.

We have a far different set of tools at hand from what Job had. We have the life and teachings of Jesus that show so much more than Job could ever see. We have the Spirit of Christ living in us (Romans 8:9), showing us, teaching us, reminding us, guiding us. We have the written Word of God, a guide that shows us both the world of Job and the world of Jesus—our world. We can face the realities of our suffering in a very different way from how Job faced his suffering.

I say, "We can face suffering in a very different way" because there are some (many?) even today who chose to live 'pre-Christian' lives as they hold on to a pre-Christian worldview, who walk in the same darkness of 'the retribution principle' that Job and his friends walked in. In fact, many professing Christians embrace the same erroneous theology of Job and his friends as they sit around in the midst of their suffering wondering, "Why is God doing this to me?" Many today have chosen to remain in that pre-Christian, karma-structured view of the world. Why?

Others of us have embraced Jesus, we have heard his voice, we have followed him, and we now live in the Christian reality. We know that suffering is part of a broken world, a sinful world. We know we do not even have to sin personally to suffer—it just comes to us for living in this brokenness. We know that there are evil forces that run contrary to God that impact our lives. And, we know that our suffering may grow out of our bad decisions or the decisions of others—the negative side of free-will.

But, we don't sit in dust and ashes. We do not blame God for the suffering in our lives. We do not wonder if God loves us or cares for us. We do not sit around in self-pity. We experience the pain, the agony at times, of suffering. But, we have a hope that carries us through. We have a Lord who walks with us. We have God's Spirit who comforts us. We have God's Word that consoles and teaches us.

On the Journey through Suffering—

My friend, Marjan, knows suffering—physical and emotional. She has experienced the ravages of chemotherapy and the emptiness and rejection of an abandoned relationship. Where does Marjan live today—in Job's world or Jesus' world? How has the suffering of life shaped her worldview and understanding of things? Is she with karma or Christ?

In our most recent conversation, Marjan was holding on to glimmers of hope. She does not believe that these things have happened to her because she is a bad person—this is not God punishing her. But she does wonder why a 'good' God doesn't rescue her, save her from the suffering in her life. She is somewhere between 'karma' and 'trust.' That is better than being stuck in the darkness and frustration of 'karma.'

Many of us have experienced or do experience suffering. With regard to suffering, where are you living? Are you living in Job's world, or in Jesus' world? Are you blaming God for everything messed up in your life? Are you convinced that God is angry at you and is punishing you for something? Or do you recognize that we live in a broken world that includes evil powers or forces, and that all of these can impact our lives—regardless of our goodness or badness?

The choice remains before us today and every day. Do we stay in Job's world, or step into Jesus' world? The move into Jesus' world is a simple yet significant an act of faith, a step of faith, or leap of faith—a determination to believe and live (act and speak and respond) in a way that grows out of embracing God's love for us, acceptance of us, and our certainty that God is not the author of our suffering but the antidote or relief for our suffering. At the very least, God is the one who can bring something good, helpful, redeeming out of suffering. We may not be healed, saved from all the suffering of life, but God is with us, and the teachings of Jesus enable us to live through the suffering without surrendering to it.

Job or Jesus? May today be your day of deciding to follow Jesus' way. May you embrace this way of seeing and being in the world, in this world of suffering.

Questions for Reflection—

1. Have you ever misunderstood something about God, and then come to a sudden realization? Do you remember how that feels?

_____
_____
_____

2. Have new understandings of God changed the way you see the world and treat others? What are some examples from your life when this has happened?

_____
_____
_____

3. Have you been living more in Job's world or more in Jesus' world with regard to suffering?

_____
_____
_____

Chapter 11
QUESTIONS REMAIN
JOB 42:7-17

We have had quite a journey through Job. We have followed Job the man from the beginning when he confidently (and erroneously) credited God with everything that happened around and to him—good and bad. We sat with him through discussions with his 'friends.' We listened with him as God responded to the accusations set before Him, all the way to Job's final response—"I cannot understand it all."

Amazingly, through all of this, Job's faith—his trust and confidence in God—has not wavered. His understanding of reality has changed, his perception of the world has changed, his understanding of God has changed, but his faith, trust, and confidence in God has remained unmovable.

Generations of readers and writers have referred to "the patience of Job;" however, Job's patience pales in comparison to God's. Rather, Job's faith—that undeterred confidence and trust in his God even as his understanding of God shifts and changes—this is what sets Job apart. In this, Job becomes a hero and model for us; in this, we can admire and learn from Job.

In fact, this whole story begins as test to see if Job will remain faithful:

> "Does Job fear God for nothing?" Satan replied. "Have you not put a hedge around him and his household and everything he has? You have blessed the work of his hands, so that his flocks and herds are spread throughout the land. But now stretch out your hand and strike everything he has, and he will surely curse you to your face." (Job 1:9-11).

After destroying Job's family and wealth, Satan comes again before God:

> "Skin for skin!" Satan replied. "A man will give all he has for his own life. But now stretch out your hand and strike his flesh and bones, and he will surely curse you to your face." (Job 2:4-5)

From the beginning, this has been a story about remaining faithful, about trusting in God—no matter the circumstances of life. Job is not a book about patience. Job is a book about trust, faith.

The End of the Story...

Let us go to the Scriptures once more as we come to the end of this journey with Job and see what we might find.

> [7]After the LORD had said these things to Job, he said to Eliphaz the Temanite, "I am angry with you and your two friends, because you have not spoken the truth about me, as my servant Job has. [8]So now take seven bulls and seven rams and go to my servant Job and sacrifice a burnt offering for yourselves. My servant Job will pray for you, and I will accept his prayer and not deal with you according to your folly. You have not spoken the truth about me, as my servant Job has." [9]So Eliphaz the Temanite, Bildad the Shuhite and Zophar

the Naamathite did what the LORD told them; and the LORD accepted Job's prayer.

^{10}After Job had prayed for his friends, the LORD restored his fortunes and gave him twice as much as he had before. ^{11}All his brothers and sisters and everyone who had known him before came and ate with him in his house....

^{12}The LORD blessed the latter part of Job's life more than the former part. He had fourteen thousand sheep, six thousand camels, a thousand yoke of oxen and a thousand donkeys. ^{13}And he also had seven sons and three daughters. ^{14}The first daughter he named Jemimah, the second Keziah and the third Keren-Happuch. ^{15}Nowhere in all the land were there found women as beautiful as Job's daughters, and their father granted them an inheritance along with their brothers.

^{16}After this, Job lived a hundred and forty years; he saw his children and their children to the fourth generation. ^{17}And, so Job died, an old man and full of years.
(Job 42:7-17)

Here, we find the bad advice of the friends brought to light, and we find the grace of God in dealing with the friends—God instructs Job as to how to make things right for his friends.

Job is surrounded once again with family, friends, and neighbors. God restores all of Job's fortunes and even gives Job a new family (honestly, I am not sure this truly compensates for the certain sense of loss in the death of his other children, but....)

He lives a long life and comes to the end of his days.

And so, the book of Job comes to a close.

Yet, as we come to the end of this journey, two questions remain, hovering in the background:

Why does God allow suffering?

When does suffering 'win'?

Question: Why Does God Allow Suffering?

We have learned that God is not the author of suffering. We have affirmed the sovereignty—the omnipotence—of God. We have affirmed the unchanging character of God (a character made clear to us in the person of Jesus). We have rejoiced in the goodness of God. This raises a very understandable question: If God is not the author of suffering, why does our good, unchanging, all-powerful God allow suffering? Why does our God allow what harms, hurts, maims or kills?

Surely, the God who spoke the world into existence could end the world's suffering with a word. Certainly, God could rescue any and all of us from our suffering in a second. Why does God allow suffering?

The answer lies in where suffering comes from. Let us look again at our working definition of suffering:

> Suffering is enduring, going through, experiencing prolonged physical, mental and/or emotional pain as a result of illness, injury and/or loss.

Suffering is a result of 'illness, injury and/or loss.' So, in order to rid the world of suffering, God would have to remove illness, injury, and loss from our lives.

"GREAT!" we would say, right? "God—do it! Get these things out of our lives!"

Yes, I would agree. But....

But, now we need to step back and ask, why do we have illness, injury, and loss in our world in the first place? Are these things that God in unparalleled wisdom simply added to our world at the time of creation? Are these some of the things that God simply included in our 'earth experience' for some odd reason?

No. No, because God is not the author of suffering.

Of course, we have to go back to the beginning—again!—to remember why we have illness, injury, and loss in our lives. We have to go back to the Garden because that is where and when all of these things come into our world.

Adam and Eve were created by God, placed in an amazing Garden that provided all of their needs and probably for all of their joys as well (see Genesis 2 and 3). Yet, God did not want people to be robots, automatons, so God gave humans the ability to choose, to decide, to rebel even—God gave humanity the gift of 'free-will.' The positive side of free-will is our ability to love, to choose to embrace God and others; the negative side of free-will is our ability to focus inward in selfishness, to reject, ignore, or even harm others.

Popular apologist and writer, C.S. Lewis, captures the importance of free-will beautifully in his book, *The Case for Christianity*:

> "God created things which had free will. That means creatures which can go wrong or right.... Why, then, did God give them free will? Because free will, though it makes evil possible, is also the only thing that makes possible any love or goodness or joy worth having.... The happiness which God designs for His higher creatures is the happiness of being freely, voluntarily united to Him and to each other in an ecstasy of love and delight compared with which the most rapturous love between a man and a woman on this

earth is mere milk and water. And for that they've got to be free." [31]

Free-will is foundational for love. When Jesus affirms that the greatest commandment is to "love the Lord your God ... and your neighbor as yourself" (Mark 12:30, 31), he basically declares love to be the foundation of our faith. With no choice, with no free-will, love is not an option. So, God creates humanity with the ability to choose—God gives us free-will.

In the Garden, God placed a tree—one tree among the hundreds if not thousands—and asked the man and woman not to eat of the fruit of that one tree. The presence of that tree served as the symbol of free-will, of freedom. Without the option to choose, there would be no freedom, no free-will, no decision to make with regard to trusting, believing, having confidence in God.

You probably remember the story of the Garden. One of those rebellious, contrary creatures was there, as in Job's narrative, but this time in the form of a serpent, urging the couple to try just a bite of the fruit from the forbidden tree: "Surely you will not die as God has suggested ... I mean, look, it's a beautiful fruit ... just one bite" (see Genesis 3). And the man and woman—in their freedom—decided not to trust God, not to believe God, to do their own thing, and they ate the fruit. They sinned. They rebelled against God's wishes and hopes and dreams for them. And in that moment, sin entered the world.

Ah. There it is: Sin—the source of all our brokenness, our pain, our illness, our injury, and our loss. Sin—it is the expression of our rebellion against God , a rebellion that is a negative result of our free-will. Free-will is our God-given ability to decide if we will trust, believe in, follow, and love God—or not.

---

[31] Lewis, C. S. *The Case for Christianity (C.S. Lewis Classics)*. (1st Touchstone Ed., Touchstone Books, 1996).

Therefore, in order for God to remove suffering from our lives, God would have to remove the effects of sin that we brought into the world. Removing sin and the possibility of sin would require removing the gift of free-will—the very thing that enables us to love God, to choose God, to follow Jesus.

If God removed only the consequences of sin today from this whole world and left with us the gift of free-will, someone—probably me...or you—would sin tomorrow (or tonight!), and the pain, loss and injury would return. The only antidote for suffering would be to remove free-will and all of the agents of free-will—humans and evil beings and powers. Without free will, we could not choose to love God, to respond to God, or to love and respond to anyone else.

Free-will remains, so suffering remains. But, the good news is that God promises to eventually set things right. In the end, God will put things right and suffering will be no more. [32]

Question: When Does Suffering Win?

Until the end, suffering is and will be part and parcel of life in this world. To remove suffering would be to remove free-will, our ability to love God and others, to decide consciously and intentionally to sacrifice our own desires for the benefit of others.

If we cannot escape suffering, then when does suffering win? When do the powers of darkness, rebellion, the negative consequences of free-will win?

Suffering does not win when we die. Paul indicates that when we die, we are then "at home with the Lord" (II Cor. 5:8). Also, Jesus, as he was dying a horrific death on the cross, consoled the repentant thief who was dying likewise beside him, "...today you will be with

---

[32] See The Revelation of John, chapters 21 and 22.

me in paradise" (Luke 23:43). No, death is not the triumph of suffering. In death, suffering loses, and we are freed from suffering to live eternity with God.

Suffering and the powers contrary to God do not win even in giving us a life-time of suffering. Paul was acquainted with suffering. He writes "...a thorn in the flesh was given to me, a messenger of Satan to buffet me..." in II Corinthians 12:7. Here, Paul, too, is very aware of where his suffering comes from: Satan. His suffering remains. Even after much prayer, the suffering remained.

Also, Jesus tells us that the life of faith is not going to be 'a walk in the park.' In the Sermon on the Mount, Jesus indicates what we may face: "Blessed are you when people insult you, persecute you and falsely say all kinds of evil against you because of me" (Matthew 5:11). Again, in the Gospel of John, Jesus intimates that life will be hard: "...In this world you will have trouble. But take heart! I have overcome the world" (John 16:33). This is a world of trouble, persecution, thorns in the flesh, pain, and suffering, but Jesus has the last word—"I have overcome the world."

So, when does suffering win? When do the powers of darkness and the principalities of this world win? When do the negative consequences of free-will win? The answer appears in Job, back in those opening chapters—where we began. Just as we had to know the end of the story to understand the beginning, we now must return to the beginning to bring things to an end.

Returning to that opening scene, we find Satan taunting God, declaring that if God would "stretch out your hand and strike everything he has, ...he will surely curse you to your face" (Job 1:11). Satan receives permission to do his foolishness, but Job does not turn his back on God.

Again, in Job 2, Satan challenges God promising that if God would "stretch out your hand and strike his flesh and bones, ...he will surely curse you to your face" (Job 2:5). Again, Satan inflicts suffering on Job, yet Job's faith remains firm.

In the face of suffering, Job remains firm in his trust in God. Job determines to remain faithful to God. Suffering and evil would have won only if Job had abandoned his faith in God.

Suffering wins and the powers of evil win and the negative consequences of free-will win when we turn our backs on God due to our suffering. As we have already mentioned, Paul in his letter to the Corinthian church declares three elements to be foundational for God's people— "these three remain: faith, hope and love…" (I Corinthian 13:13). Suffering wins when we allow the suffering of our lives to rob us of our faith in God—our trust in the goodness of God, in the presence of God. Suffering wins when we relinquish hope, when we refuse to see possibility, when we close our eyes and our minds to something or someplace better than where we are. Suffering wins when we allow the pain of our situation to make us blind to the people around us, when we no longer care about anyone else, when we cease to love.

Suffering wins when we exchange faith for doubt and distrust, when we let go of hope and cling to inevitability and cold determinism, when we abandon love in favor of selfishness, self-centeredness, and self-pity. When we hold on to trust, possibility, and the value and importance of others beyond ourselves, suffering and all the powers that cause it to lose.

Suffering on its Head

So, God will not take suffering out of this world. If God did, we would turn around tomorrow, sin again, and we would have the suffering back! So, what does God do with our suffering?

We learned a few chapters back from the apostle Paul that "suffering produces perseverance, perseverance character, and character hope." That is one positive thing the God does with suffering—God uses the suffering in our lives to produce hope, to help us to reach farther, to look beyond where we are.

God also uses suffering to temper us a bit. When we see the suffering incurred by those who do not take care of themselves, those who have delved into the world of drugs and alcohol abuse, those who have elected to live on the wild side of violence, those who have lived egocentric and self-destructive lives—when we see their suffering and/or the suffering endured by their families and loved ones, we are less likely to embrace those kinds of lives. Suffering in others can move us away from destructive behaviors and dangerous situations.

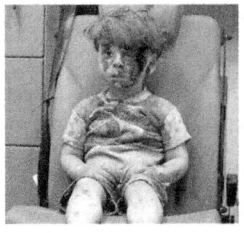

And, suffering expands our humanity. How many of us saw this picture (right) of the little boy in Aleppo, Syria, sitting in the back of the ambulance during the Syrian civil war? [33] When we see his suffering, we are moved. We feel for the people of Syria who endure these horrors.

Many of us have seen devastation in parts of the United States due to the flooding, hurricanes, droughts, and fires. People living in these areas endure long-term pain from loss. They suffer. When we see their suffering, our hearts are softened, and we are moved to help, to reach out. Indeed, many of us have given above and beyond to help the people of various countries, states, and communities in their times of need, in the midst of their suffering. We have responded to hurricanes, tornados, wildfires, earthquakes, house-fires, and more. Suffering expands our compassion.

---

[33] BBC News. "Omran Daqneesh, Aleppo's Bloodied Boy, Shown in New Images." *BBC News*, 6 June 2017, www.bbc.com/news/world-middle-east-40176781.

We would be amiss to discuss suffering and not turn to Victor Frankl, the great 20th Century psychologist, philosopher, and Holocaust survivor. He was acutely familiar with suffering as he lost his wife, his parents, and his brothers to German concentration camps in World War II. And, he himself suffered but survived Auschwitz and Dachau "death camps." As a psychologist, he both experienced and simultaneously examined his experiences, and he later wrote about it all in his famous work, *Man's Search for Meaning* (1959).

In this work, Frankl argues persuasively that "there must be meaning in suffering. Suffering is an ineradicable part of life, even as fate and death. Without suffering and death human life cannot be complete."[34] Frankl's experiences and his work in psychology taught him that suffering is part of the human condition, that suffering somehow makes us human. He also recognizes that suffering actually provides meaning to life:

> The way in which a man [sic] accepts his fate and the suffering it entails, the way in which he takes up his cross, gives him ample opportunity...to add a deeper meaning to his life. It may remain brave, dignified and unselfish. Or in the bitter fight for self-preservation he may forget his human dignity and become no more than an animal. Here lies the chance for a man either to make use of or forego the opportunities of attaining the moral values that a difficult situation may afford him.[35]

According to Frankl, suffering provides an opportunity to live into our humanity, provides something that allows us find meaning. When we allow our suffering to grow our compassion and to point us towards others, this becomes very true. In life, in my life, we find that our suffering does enable us to help others. When we see

---

[34] Victor Frankl. *Man's Search for Meaning*. (Boston, Mass: Beacon Press, 2006.) 67.
[35] Ibid.

someone suffering as we have suffered—illness, injury, or loss—we can feel for and with the person now going through suffering.

In one congregation we served, I recall watching one family go through the loss of the husband and father to cancer. The son, only 14-years-old, was really struggling, trying so hard to be 'a man,' to endure. When I was 17 years old, my own father died of cancer, and I, too, struggled a lot. Having truly suffered through this kind of loss gave me the opportunity to sit with this teenager on several occasions and commiserate with him, to share with him the feelings I had struggled with. Drawing on my experience through the same type of suffering, we were able to "connect." We talked, we cried, we sat in silence, and then we even found space for laughter. Our suffering means that our humanity, our empathy, is expanded. God can enable us to use our suffering to help others who suffer as we have suffered.

God takes suffering and makes it a positive force in our lives. Even in suffering, God's Word remains true and faithful:

> And we know that all things work together for good to those who love God, to those who are the called according to His purpose.   (Romans 8:28, NKJV)

All things. All things work together. All things work together for good. Even suffering. We may not see it at the time; we may think that the world is over, life is over, love is over, but God can and will use every broken, ugly, life-robbing thing Satan and evil powers and other people throw at us to strengthen us or to strengthen someone else. God can even use the suffering from our foolish, self-destructive behaviors to bring about something good.

The Cross

There is no place that we see suffering turned on its head more clearly than in the Cross.

Suffering? Jesus suffered—like we cannot imagine. Those passages in Luke's Gospel where Jesus sets his sights on Jerusalem even though he knows he is going there to suffer always give me pause. He even tells his disciples that he is going to suffer (see Luke 9:22, 17:25, and 22:15.)

In those final days, Jesus endures public ridicule, beatings, a crown of thorns, and finally the most horrific form of execution the Romans could think of—crucifixion: Public humiliation as one is hung naked before the world; physical pain as nails pierce flesh and break bone, as the muscles exhaust themselves and the person slowly suffocates to death. Crucifixion was designed to be a slow, painful, dignity-robbing death—a suffering death.

God could have saved Jesus from this death, but God knew that only through this suffering death could we—you and I—be saved from the power of sin over our lives. In Jesus' death, you and I discover the power of faith, come to know the meaning of hope, and see the very face of love.

On the Journey through Suffering—

The Eucharistic implications of all this are huge. Too often, we have come to the Communion table with long faces. Too long, the gathering of God's people at the table has been a solemn affair. Too long, we have come with a 'woe is me' attitude that has robbed the moment of the power that Jesus infused in the moment. We often forget—or perhaps never realized—that the Passover dinner was a celebration, a time of thanksgiving and joy as the Jewish people remembered and celebrated the providence of God in rescuing them from Egypt—from lives of suffering.

As we Christians come to the Communion table 'as often' as we may, we must come with thankful hearts—through Jesus' suffering, our sins are forgiven, we are given life, God's love is revealed. We must come with joy—through Jesus' subsequent resurrection, we have hope for that day when all things will be made new, when we see the reality of eternal life.

As we prepare to come to that table in the future, let us consider anew the suffering that God endured through Jesus, and give thanks that God has redeems even the suffering of our lives. May our faith, like that of Job, remain ever constant. May we recognize that our good, unchanging, all-powerful God is ever working all things together for good. Because, besides being amazingly patient, God is good ... all the time. May these three remain ever the bedrock of our lives: faith, hope, and love. As long as we hold on to these, suffering cannot win.

Questions for Reflection—

1. Have you seen God turn suffering on its head? Have you seen something good and positive come out of a situation of suffering?

_____
_____
_____

2. Have you considered Communion or the Lord's Supper a joyful occasion? Can you see how it could be?

_____
_____
_____

3. Do you think you will face suffering—yours and others'—differently now that you have this new reading of Job?

_____
_____
_____

Chapter 12
CLOSING THOUGHTS
...GOD WITH US

As John Wesley, the founder of the Methodist movement, was coming to the end of his life, as he lay in bed the night of his death, he uttered his last words: "And the best of all—God with us." [36]

Like the doctrines of God's sovereignty (God is all-powerful) and the Trinity (God and Jesus and the Holy Spirit are one), the doctrine of God's presence is also incredibly important—especially when it comes to the theme of suffering.

Recently, I was reminded yet again that God does not take away the suffering of our lives, but God is with us through the suffering. This reminder came at a funeral for a young man who was senselessly taken from family and friends by an automobile accident. The minister at the service of remembrance pointed out something from one of the most well-known psalms, Psalm 23:

> Yea, though I walk through the valley of the shadow of death, I will fear no evil: for thou art with me; thy rod and thy staff they comfort me. (Psalm 23:4, KJV)

---

[36] Michael Youssef. "Final Words." *Leading The Way with Dr. Michael Youssef*, 28 Feb. 2021, www.ltw.org/read/my-devotional/2021/02/final-words.

In this Psalm of comfort, in these words that bring calm and peace to so many people in times of grief, God does not snatch the person out of the "valley of the shadow of death." Rather, the promise is to be with the person through the valley, the promise is to comfort the person in the midst of their difficult time. This is a promise we can hold on to as well.

We find this promise of God's presence in our lives throughout the Scriptures. In the Old Testament, we find these words of promise:

> The LORD himself goes before you and will be with you;
> he will never leave you nor forsake you. Do not be afraid;
> do not be discouraged." (Deuteronomy 31:8)

> Have I not commanded you? Be strong and courageous.
> Do not be afraid; do not be discouraged, for the LORD
> your God will be with you wherever you go."
> (Joshua 1:9)

> So do not fear, for I am with you;
> do not be dismayed, for I am your God.
> I will strengthen you and help you;
> I will uphold you with my righteous right hand.
> (Isaiah 41:10)

This same message of presence is all through the New Testament as well. In Matthew's Gospel, we are reminded before Jesus is born that Jesus will be "Immanuel (which means 'God with us')" (Matt. 1:23). When Jesus comes to the end of his ministry and sends out his disciples to "all nations," he promises them, "I am with you always" (Matt. 28:20).

Paul speaks directly to the issues of suffering and pain and loss in this world in his letter to the Roman church:

> For I am convinced that neither death nor life, neither
> angels nor demons, neither the present nor the future,

nor any powers, neither height nor depth, nor anything else in all creation, will be able to separate us from the love of God that is in Christ Jesus our Lord.
(Romans 8:38-39.)

And Jesus, speaking not only of God's presence in our lives, reminds us that in the Church, the gathering of God's people—whether two people or two thousand people—God is there, present:

For where two or three gather in my name, there am I with them. (Matt. 18:20)

God is with us. In the midst of our suffering, our loss, our pain, God is with us. Whether we suffer a broken heart or a broken leg, God is with us. Whether we lose a job or lose a limb, God is with us. If we are robbed of peace or robbed of possessions, God is still with us. When a dream dies or a loved one dies, God is with us, for us, beside us, within us, wanting to walk with us through the pains of this world, desiring to bring comfort in our pain and suffering ... if we will allow God to do so. But it is so hard to allow God to do this if we think God is the source of our suffering.

In my experience as a pastor, I have too often seen people abandon God and the Church when suffering comes along. People are quick to blame God for their suffering. How many times I have seen a man or woman, sometimes an entire family, abandon the church when their spouse or loved one dies. They are angry at God for the loss; they blame God for the suffering of their lives. So, they walk away from God, and they walk away from the church—they walk away from the One who wants more than anything to walk with them through the pain, and they abandon the very people who want to be with them through their time of hurt and loss.

If this book does little else, I hope it will help you to see that God is not the source of suffering, and that God and the church want to be with you in your times of suffering—in your pain, hurt, and loss.

How do we respond to this God who is with us? We find comfort and strength through prayers for help and prayers of complaint (David has many of these in the Psalms)—whether uttered as a whisper in the quiet of our apartment or shouted to the universe under a starry sky. We find hope and peace through reading about God—whether in the Bible or in other words written by faithful followers of God. We find encouragement and relief when we gather with others—whether in God's Church or with "two or three" friends who truly care for and love us. In these ways and more, whether we "feel" it or not, we embrace "God with us," and we are strengthened for the journey.

* * *

In the opening pages of this work, I quoted one my literary heroes, James Martin, SJ:

> "The best answer to 'Why do we suffer?' may be 'We don't know.' Anyone who offers you 'the answer' is either a liar or a fool. And has probably never faced real suffering." [37]

Perhaps I am a fool. Perhaps I have not yet experienced the level of suffering that gives me license to speak to the greater issues of suffering in this world. Job, however, has experienced pain and suffering the likes of which probably none of us has encountered. Job has guided us on this journey, and the book that carries his name has helped us discover so much along the way. If Job has not taught us everything, the readings have pointed us to Jesus who has answered so many of our questions.

I do not believe I am a liar. I hope and pray that I have faithfully dealt with both the book of Job and the life of Job. I hope that the connections I have seen in Scripture from the Old Testament and

---

[37] James Martin, JS. "Why is There Suffering?" *The Way of Suffering: Readings for an Enlightened Life*. James Leach et al, eds. (Maryknoll, NY: Orbis Books, 2020) 9.

New Testament, that I have brought to bear in this reading of Job and applied to the theme of suffering, are faithful interpretations and applications.

Job suffered financial ruin. He suffered the deaths of those who were closest to him. He suffered illness and disease. He suffered in every way that we may suffer, and he suffered them all at the same time. We may lose a job or fall on financially hard times. We may face the death of a loved one, the loss of someone so dear to us. We may face illness or disease—temporary or terminal. But we usually do not face them all at the same time. Job takes us on a journey through all of the sufferings that life can throw at us.

My dear friend, Marjan, still suffers—her journey through suffering is not yet over. At the time of publication of the first edition of this book (August 2021), she had just undergone radical surgery that left her physically changed forever. She was unsure of the future—she did not know where her life was going, where she would be even a year from then. Where is Marjan today?

She suffers still.

Physically, the return to 'normal,' to full health is slow. Two years ago, she underwent a radical, double mastectomy after six months of intensive chemotherapy. Coming back from that is not an easy task. Today, she does not have a lot of energy, but she continues her studies. She is looking for work, but even driving leaves her dizzy—so she looks for something she can walk to. She has one year of college left, and she will have her bachelor's degree. What's next?

I asked Marjan about her hopes and dreams. She told me that people who have had 'near death experiences' often do not think of long-term dreams. The present becomes so important because they know that the future is not guaranteed. So, Marjan focuses on the next 1-6 months—no further.

I pressed her on the question—is there anything in the long-term? The most she can dream for today: A job—30 hours a week, her own apartment ("Just a small one…"), and to finish her studies. So, even though her experiences hold her back from any sort of long-term plans, she does see where she is, sees where she would like to be, and she is doing what she can to get there.

Job's story has a "happily ever after" ending—fortunes and family are restored and all is made as right as possible. Marjan's story has not yet gotten there. While her cancer is behind her, she still suffers—dreams unfilled, loneliness, uncertainty about the future. While she faces an uncertain future, there is hope. I also sense love in her life—meaningful, self-giving relationships are forming. Her compassion grows. A faith in God? A trust in a good God working "all things together for good"? We are working on that. Until she is there, I will believe for her even as I hoped for her when she had no hope. Our conversations continue.

* * *

In this brief work on a topic that has filled thousands of books over the centuries, we have attempted to answer a few questions: Where does suffering come from? What do we do with suffering—in our lives and the lives of others? Why does God allow suffering? When does suffering 'win'?

My hope is that you have found some answers to these questions, answers that will better enable you to live with and through the suffering of this world.

In my experience as a minister, I have too often seen people abandon God and the church when life-altering suffering comes their way. If this book does little else, I hope it will help all to see that God is not the source of our suffering, that God and God's church want to help us through.

While some questions may remain unanswered, my hope in all of this is that Job has been able to show us what suffering is—something contrary to God's wishes for us, something that powers of evil, our own selfishness and self-destructive behaviors, and the brokenness world has brought upon us.

In response to the suffering in our lives and the world around us, may we remain faithful to God—trusting in the midst of the hurt and losses in our lives. May we be faithful friends who sit with those who suffer, who pray for those who suffer, who allow those who suffer to express their pain. May we see that suffering can lead us to hope, and hope can lead us to new places along the journey. May we learn from suffering—ours and others'—and may we use our experiences in suffering to help others in their suffering. Finally, may we know that God longs to walk with us through our suffering, to strengthen us, to comfort us.

We know and understand that suffering 'wins' only when we allow it to rob us of our faith and confidence in God, when we allow it to steal our hope for a better future, and when we allow it to take away our love for others. As Job has modeled for us, may we weather whatever suffering in this life with an unwavering trust in the goodness and presence of God. May we remain faithful, hopeful, and loving through all our journeys in life.

The End

Bibliography

Clines, David J. A. *Word Biblical Commentary: Job 1-20*. Zondervan, 1989.

David Crowder Band. "David Crowder*Band - How He Loves (Official Music Video)." YouTube, uploaded by davidcrowderband, 14 Oct. 2009, www.youtube.com/watch?v=TCunuL58odQ.

Frankl, Victor. *Man's Search for Meaning*. Boston, Mass: Beacon Press, 2006.

Hartley, J.E. "Job." *International Standard Bible Encyclopedia, Vol. II*. William B.. Erdmann's Publishing Co: Grand Rapids, MI. 1982.

Herrin, Jon A. *Making Sense of It All: Reflections on the Ancient Narratives of Genesis*. KDP Publishing, 2020.

Holy Bible, King James Version. Thomas Nelson, 2018.

Holy Bible, New King James Version. Thomas Nelson, 2005.

Kluger, Jeffrey. "How Hope Works." TIME.Com, 7 Mar. 2013, healthland.time.com/2013/03/07/this-is-your-mind-on-hope.

Kristof, Nicholas. "Opinion | The Power of Hope Is Real." *The New York Times*, 21 May 2015, www.nytimes.com/2015/05/21/opinion/nicholas-kristof-the-power-of-hope-is-real.html.

Kushner, Aviya. *The Grammar of God: A Journey into the Words and Worlds of the Bible*. First Edition, Random House, 2015.

Lewis, C. S. *The Case for Christianity* (C.S. Lewis Classics). 1st Touchstone Ed, Touchstone Books, 1996.

"Major Background Issues from the Ancient Near East," NIV Cultural Backgrounds Study Bible, Craig S. Keener and John H. Walton, eds. Grand Rapids, MI: Zondervan Publishers, 2016.

Martin, James, JS. "Why is There Suffering?" *The Way of Suffering: Readings for an Enlightened Life*. James Leach et al, eds. Maryknoll, NY: Orbis Books, 2020.

Merritt, Jonathan. "Some of the Most Visible Christians in America are Failing the Coronavirus Test." *The Atlantic*, April 24, 2020, https://www.theatlantic.com/ideas/archive/2020/04/christian-cruelty-face-covid-19/610477/ .

"Narrative FAQ." Working Preacher from Luther Seminary, Luther Seminary, 18 Apr. 2021, www.workingpreacher.org/narrative-faq.

Oxford University Press (OUP). "Lament." Lexico.Com, 2021, www.lexico.com/en/definition/lament.

Peterson, Eugene. *The Message New Testament with Psalms and Proverbs*. 1st ed., NavPress Publishing Group, 2007.

Radford, Benjamin. "Human Lifespans Nearly Constant for 2,000 Years." Livescience.Com, 21 Aug. 2009, www.livescience.com/10569-human-lifespans-constant-2-000-years.html.

Redmond, Matt. "Blessed Be Your Name." YouTube. https://www.youtube.com/watch?v=du0il6d-DAk.

Reuters. "Beirut Explosion Rocks Bride's Photoshoot." YouTube, uploaded by Reuters, 5 Aug. 2020, www.youtube.com/watch?v=_L7SlqDtRnc.

Seger, Patrick. "The Power of Hope." Samaritan's Purse, 24 Dec. 2013, www.samaritanspurse.org/article/the-power-of-hope.

"Suicide Machines." Dr. Jack Kevorkian: Euthanasia and Physician Assisted Suicide, 2012, euthanasian.weebly.com/suicide-machines.html.

The Holy Bible: New International Version. Grand Rapids, Michigan, Zondervan, 2011.

"Theodicy." Merriam-Webster.com Dictionary, Merriam-Webster, https://www.merriam-webster.com/dictionary/theodicy. Accessed 1 May. 2021.

Weatherhead, Leslie D. *The Will of God*. New York: Abingdon-Cokesbury Press, 1944.

Youssef, Michael. "Final Words." *Leading The Way with Dr. Michael Youssef*, 28 Feb. 2021, www.ltw.org/read/my-devotional/2021/02/final-words.

ABOUT THE AUTHOR

While born in south Alabama, Herrin left the US when he was just turning four-years-old. His parents—missionaries Manget and Elaine Herrin—raised Jon and his two brothers in Guyana, South America, and on the island of Grenada in the West Indies. After coming to the US when he was turning seventeen years old, he studied English in university (B.A., M.A.T.). While in graduate school the first time around, Jon met his wife, Jeanne. From grad school, Herrin went on to become an Asst. Prof. of English.

While being a life-long educator (college, university, and seminary; teacher and administrator), Jon is also an ordained minister in the United Methodist Church. Having studied theology and the Bible extensively (M.T.S., M.Div., Th.M., Th.D.), he enjoys teaching and preaching in the Church and the Academy. Jon presently serves as the lead pastor of the McAllen First United Methodist Church. Jon's calling is to help others know God and to live life with joy.

With his wife, Jeanne, and three children, Jon lived and served in both Venezuela and Mexico over the course of seven years in international mission service. Jon and Jeanne have settled in the Rio Grande Valley of south Texas, on the US/Mexico border, where they love the culture, food, and climate...and the slower speed of life.

Herrin's hobbies and happy places include reading, teaching, hiking, and espresso.

Follow Jon here: www.jonherrinwriter.com.
    Contact Jon here: jonherrinwriter@gmail.com.
        Jon is available for speaking and teaching events.

Previous works include: *Making Sense of It All: Reflections of the Ancient Narratives of Genesis* (2020), *A Journey through Suffering: A New Reading of Job in the 21st Century* (2021), and *Genesis for Today: Redeeming Ancient Narratives for Contemporary Living* (2023).

(Available at Amazon.com and BarnesandNoble.com)

Notes

Made in the USA
Coppell, TX
26 December 2025

67303207R10098